A Future, A Hope, An Expected End

The Inevitable Conquest of Christianity

Wayne Rohde

© 2001 by Wayne Rohde

A Future, A Hope, An Expected End
by Wayne Rohde

Printed in the United States of America
ISBN 1-931232-17-2

All rights reserved. No part of this publication may be reproduced or transmitted in any form or by any means without written permission of the publisher.

Unless otherwise indicated, all scripture quotations are taken from the *Holy Bible*, Authorized King James Version, copyright © 1985, 1983 by Thomas Nelson, Inc.

Additional Translations Used and Noted:

(NKJV) *The Holy Bible*, New King James Version, copyright © 1982 by Thomas Nelson, Inc.

(NIV) New International Version, copyright © 1973 by the New York Bible Society International.

Scripture quotations marked (NLT) are taken from the *Holy Bible*, New Living Translation, copyright © 1996. Used by permission of Tyndale House Publishers, Inc., Wheaton, Illinois 60189.

Xulon Press
11350 Random Hill Center
Suite 800
Fairfax, VA 22030
(703) 279-6511
XulonPress.com

Dedication

This book is dedicated to my daughters, Nicole and Kristy, and my grandchildren, Bethany and Seth, who will, by the grace of God, enter the future and expand the Kingdom of God.

Acknowledgments

This book would not have been possible without the freedom and support provided by the fine people of the church I pastor, Jubilee Christian Family Church in Milwaukee, WI.

A few of those people are worthy of special mention. Frank Krzeminski, Mike Skott and Kathie Lingafelt provided constant encouragement in writing the manuscript. Colleen Skott and Art Chavez, who spent many hours in proof reading and editing. Special thanks are due to my pastor, Dr. Mark T. Barclay, for his suggestions for making this book more palatable to a wider base of readers. Thanks to Rev. Kenneth Foreman for help in the final editing of the manuscript. And finally, thanks to Rev. David Mallonee, who encouraged me originally and repeatedly over the last six years to write this book.

Foreword

I consider it a privilege to be asked to write the forward to this book. I encouraged Brother Wayne to write this book some time ago and not because the Body of Christ needed more books. I felt he could write from a perspective which would enlighten a very specific group of people.

I am glad he took his time in preparation for this work. A book worthy of the Body of Christ takes years to be ready for public consumption (haste makes waste). This is a volume you will refer to again and again.

The content in this book has the potential to revolutionize your life and ministry, as it has mine. Every major decision we make in life is influenced by what we believe about the second coming. I had been taught along the lines of current "pop" eschatology and I made decisions because of that teaching I now regret. I simply never heard the other side of the story.

I encourage you to read with an open mind. The admonition to, "search the scriptures", is always appropriate. As you read through this book, one of two things will happen. Either you will be strengthened in your current viewpoint, or you will discover fresh truth which will positively alter the rest of your life.

Happy reading!

Rev. David Mallonee
Concepts In Stewardship
Rogersville, MO

Contents

Chapter 1: Introduction 1
What's The Problem? 4
A Better Solution 4
What Happened To Hope? 5
Wagonloads of Evidence 6
Ideas Have Consequences 9
How Did We Get Here? 10
A Challenge To The Reader 11

Chapter 2: Darby & Company 13
Amillennialism 14
Classical Premillennialism 15
Postmillennialism 17
Darby & Dispensational
    Premillennialism 20
Who Puffed Darby? 25

Chapter 3: The Mysterious Gap 31
Daniel's Seventy Weeks 32
Darby's Parenthesis 34
The Gap Disappears 35
Daniel's Perspective of Time 38

Chapter 4: The Fifth Kingdom 41
Daniel's Interpretation 42
The Fifth Kingdom 44
The Dispensational Problem 46

A Future, A Hope, An Expected End

Chapter 5:	How Many Resurrections? 49
	Only One Resurrection 50
	Follow The Rules! 54
	What The Fathers Said 55

Chapter 6:	How Short Is Shortly? 57
	Shortly Means Soon..................................58
	To Seal Or Not To Seal? 60
	What About the "Last Days?" 63

Chapter 7:	A Relevant Revelation..................................69
	In This Generation 70
	It Is Finished 75
	In The Tribulation 77
	The Antichrist 79

Chapter 8:	When Will These Things Be? 87
	The Setting For Jesus' Prophecy 88
	The Three Questions..................................91
	The Time Stamp...92
	What Would They See? 93
	Signs of the Times 95
	Specific Warnings and Instructions 105
	Time To Escape! 107
	A Darkened Sun?.....................................109
	A Final Time Stamp................................111
	An Incredible Parallel 112
	The Last Question 113
	Who Is Left Behind?................................114
	His Final Answer 116

Chapter 9:	The Prophets Have Spoken 117
	What Does The Millennium Look Like?...118
	How Does The "Garden" Grow?.............122
	Where Is Christ? 123

Contents

Chapter 10: A Future, A Hope, An Expected End 127
          Possessing the Gate of the Enemy............129
          Philosophies Do Have Consequences!....131
          Destined To Win!......................................133
          Great Expectations...................................134

Selected Bibliography..135

CHAPTER 1

Introduction

Proverbs 18:17

He that is first in his own cause seemeth just; but his neighbor cometh and searcheth him. (KJV)

Any story sounds true until someone sets the record straight. (NLT)

A few years ago I discovered a *"fresh"* truth which rattled my rather rigid theological paradigms. For that reason, was difficult for me to accept at first. By *"fresh"* I mean it is *fresh to me, not to the Church*. In fact, as I found out, it was the historical position of the Church until early in the nineteenth century. The truth I discovered was a view of eschatology (the study of end time events), that I had never before heard of.

While I was struggling with accepting the position, which

was contrary to the doctrine I had believed and taught publically for many years, I encountered this statement: *"There is a principle which is a bar against all information, which is a proof against all arguments and cannot fail to keep a man or woman in everlasting ignorance. This principle is **contempt prior to investigation**."* This is in accord with what the scripture declares in Prov. 18:13, *"He who answers a matter before he heareth it, it is a folly and a shame unto him."*

I resolved then and there, to determine what the Word of God teaches concerning end time events, to conduct an open minded study using the scriptures, rather than what I had been taught and believed. I pray you will apply the same principle as you read this book and discover "new" truth that may be contrary to what you have previously learned and accepted. If you disagree you will have lost nothing and your confidence in your current belief will be strengthened. If you agree a whole new realm of faith and life will be opened to you. Don't be afraid to put your belief system to the test. Such tests often produce new realms of faith and victory.

The rallying cry of the Reformation was *"Ecclesia reformata quia semper reformada est,"* meaning, *"The church reformed because it must always be reforming."* The Reformation shook the religious world because the Reformers were willing to examine church teaching and tradition in light of the sacred scriptures and then cast out traditional sacred cows in favor of revealed truth. Would to God that we today would be as willing to examine our theological footings and repair them as necessary!

Doctrine does have consequences. What you believe about the end times effects what you do now. If things are

Introduction

only going to get worse until Christ returns, then why have children, why send your children to a Christian school, plan for retirement or be involved in political or social action if Christ is returning within a few years?

This issue became very real to me in 1978 as I considered attending Bible school to prepare for the ministry. At that time Hal Lindsay and others were predicting the "Rapture" in 1981.[1] Why attend Bible school if you will never get to minister? Fortunately, despite the fact that I believed Lindsay, by the grace of God I did decide to go and have now been in the ministry for over twenty years.

Now to put the ball in your court. How will you respond if you learn you are embracing a teaching that was not believed by any of the early Church or Church fathers including Origen, Eusebius, Athanasius or Augustine? What if your present belief was rebuffed by Puritans including Thomas Goodwin, John Owen and John Cotton and all the great ministers of the Reformation, including John Wycliffe, John Knox, John Calvin, John and Charles Wesley, Jonathan Edwards, George Whitfield, Charles Spurgeon and many others? Further, what if the teaching you believe to be true was not endorsed by a single Protestant before the 1830s? Would you ignore these serious concerns, or would you at least want to be like a Berean and *"search the scriptures daily to find out whether these things were so?"* To help you in doing so, using the light provided by the Scriptures, is the object of this book.

---

[1] According to their scheme, Israel was regathered from the nations in 1948. Since a generation was forty years, the Lord would *have to return* before 1988. Allowing seven years for the Tribulation set the "Rapture" for 1981.

A Future, A Hope, An Expected End

What's The Problem?

The popular current end-time theology (called "dispensational premillennialism"), which is held by almost all the fundamental, evangelical and charismatic community, predicts that the world is destined to become worse and worse, leading up to the Rapture of the Church, which, according to this position, is due to happen very soon. The consequence of this view of the end times is that the culture is abandoned (*"God says it will get worse and worse!"*). Further, many Christians plan only for the short term (*"He's coming SOON!"*), and relegate the future to the world and the devil, rather than laying hold of it for Christ and future generations. The philosophy becomes a self fulfilling prophecy of defeat as the Church retreats from its God-given calling to "occupy" and of being "salt and light."

The problem will become more acute as we enter the new millennium. Already we are hearing dates regularly set and passing unfulfilled. With the avid promotion of Hal Lindsay of *Late Great Planet Earth* fame, as well as Tim LaHaye and Jerry Jenkins, authors of the wildly popular *Left Behind* series of books, stark warnings of the coming Rapture and Tribulation are becoming more shrill. As a consequence, church attendance may even increase for a time, with many wanting to take out "fire insurance," but with fear rather than faith as a motivation. When the predicted time comes and goes with no Rapture, those on the "fire escape" will leave as quickly as they came in. Worse, they will now have been "inoculated" against the truth of Church and the Word of God, believing them to be unreliable.

A Better Solution

The alternative, and the antidote to this scenario, is for the

Introduction

Church to again embrace the Biblically taught, historic view of end-time events. This position expects that the Church *will* carry out the Great Commission *in history* and, instead of the Church being rescued at the last moment from the clutches of the Antichrist, the Church will, with Christ reigning from Heaven, put all His enemies under His feet, and win the nations prior to His physical return and the final judgment. It is the inevitable victory predicted by the scriptures!

Recently, I delivered a series of messages on this subject at the church where I serve as pastor. I wondered what the effect would be, since I had always taught *(and taught well!)* the dispensational, premillennial position. I was quite pleasantly surprised to find out not only that it didn't split the church, but that the congregation received the teaching warmly. Most actually took the time to check out what I said and found it to be historically and theologically accurate.

But by far the best result was that many became motivated to plan for the future with an eye toward building the Kingdom of God. Some decided to have children. Others decided to examine changing careers. Many decided to look further into the future to plan for things they had not thought of before. And the underlying thought was, "What part can I play in advancing the Kingdom of God within my sphere of influence?" After all, regardless of our eschatology, isn't that what we are supposed to be doing?

What Happened To Hope?

The message of most evangelical and charismatic churches is almost universally one of victory in Christ over the world, the flesh and the devil. Curiously, this triumphant message does not extend into the eschatology of churches that have embraced the Trojan horse of dispensational premillennialism. Rather, they *expect* the world to become worse and worse until it becomes necessary for the Lord Himself to return and put things back in proper order. Although they believe the Christian is to overcome in life personally, this personal victory does not extend to the Church overcoming in the culture. It is my desire that this book, by the grace of God, will change this attitude.

What I'm about to present is no new doctrine, as you will see, but the classical position of the Church from its origin in the 1st century until the 1830s, when a new and previously unheard of doctrine was embraced by selected Protestants. What you will find out is that Jesus is now reigning in Heaven and expects His Church to conquer all His enemies *in history* before He physically returns to judge the quick and the dead. The Church will not be delivered at the last second from the jaws of the wicked and the devil, but instead, with the aid of the Holy Spirit, will put all His enemies under His feet! You will learn about the biblical and historical eschatology of victory!

Wagonloads of Evidence

"...When he saw the wagons which Joseph had sent to carry him, the spirit of Jacob their father revived:..." (Gen. 45:27) When Jacob saw the wagons, the evidence of Joseph's existence, he was revived and invigorated. *There are wagonloads of evidence which refute the dispensational position* and support the triumph of Christ and His Church in history. If the saying *"A chain is only as strong as its weakest link"* is applied to dispensationalism, it becomes readily apparent that the chain has no strength at all. In this book we will consider the numerous weak links of dispen-

Introduction

sational premillennialism.

The weakest link is the author of the doctrine, John Nelson Darby. Most believers have no idea that the eschatology they espouse originated in the early 1830s with the founder of the Plymouth Brethren church. Darby's "revelation" shocked the church of his day, which believed that Christ was going to return only after the faithful Church had subdued the world. An entire chapter will be devoted to Darby and how his obscure doctrine managed to gain the attention and following of the church.

Another flawed link involves *"the gap"* between the sixty-ninth and seventieth weeks of Daniel mentioned in chapter nine, first proposed by Darby. Somehow he invented a *"gap"* (which at this time it has spanned almost two thousand years) where none exists. This error is foundational to the existence of the entire doctrine. Remove it and the whole dispensational house of cards falls. You will see clearly from the scriptures that, just as in mathematics, *seventy follows immediately after sixty-nine*.

Another weak link of the chain is the supposition that an Antichrist *will come* who will rule the world from a revived Roman empire. As you will see, this flies in the face of the book of Daniel, which absolutely states that neither Rome (or any other nation) will ever again rule the world in any form. Rather, Daniel was told that the Kingdom of God would begin during the time of Rome and would (like leaven) expand until it filled the whole earth.

The Church has roots in history. All sound doctrine can be traced back to its origins in the early Church. Unfortunately this is not true of dispensationalism, with no credible proponents before Darby proposed his new doctrine in the 1830s. Are we to believe that not even Peter or Paul knew anything about this doctrine, nor did the Church Fathers, nor did the Puritans or Reformers? You will observe even the treasured historic creeds of the Church, created to preserve doctrinal orthodoxy, speak distinctly and clearly against dispensationalism.

Adding to the expanding chain of weak links is the prediction of multiple *"raptures"* or removing of the saints. Four to seven *"raptures"* are taught, depending on which version (and there are many) of this doctrine you happen to hear. You will see that the Bible teaches *only one rapture* and that it takes place *at the end of history.* This is consistent with God's pattern in history of *preserving the saints* and *removing the wicked through death.* "The righteous shall never be removed: but the wicked shall not inhabit the earth." (Prov. 10:30)

Finally, the last and fatal link to be subjected to biblical stress testing is Darby's faulty scheme of scriptural and prophetic interpretation. *All prophecies have a time context.* They are to be *specifically* and *literally* fulfilled in time and space. That is not to say that some of the principles taught by the prophecies are not repeated in later generations. For example, Isaiah spoke to his generation about events that were to effect them because of their conduct. But they still speak to us today. But great error can result if you ignore the time context of the prophecies. This is what has happened with the teaching of the premillennial Rapture and the physical millennial reign of Christ on earth. *What has already been fulfilled is being taught as if it is yet to be fulfilled.*

As you will see, this includes the Great Tribulation (it has already occurred), the identity of the Antichrist (that's right, he has already lived and died) and the time and length of the Millennium (we are in it *now*). You will also see that the

Book of Revelation was *written to the generation that was living when it was written*, not a generation two thousand or more years in the future.

Ideas Have Consequences

Why is eschatology important? Quite simply: *philosophies have consequences*. The Early Church believed the prophecy concerning the imminent destruction of Jerusalem and sold their property and provided relief for their brethren. History tells us not a single Christian died in that great destruction warned about by Jesus in the gospels and Revelation. Kenneth L. Gentry Jr. has summed it up well on the cover of his book, *He Shall Have Dominion*.

> *Two centuries ago, Protestant Christians believed that they would die before Jesus came back to earth. This affected the way they thought, prayed, worked and saved. They built for the future. They were future-oriented. They were upper-class. Today, many Protestants believe that Jesus is coming back soon, so they will not have to die. This belief affects the way they think, pray, work and save. They are present-oriented. They are lower-class.*[2]

Because the church has embraced Darby's invention she has given up her hope of winning the world for Christ. She has in effect said, *"If the Church is leaving shortly, and the prophets say things must get worse and worse, why should I*

---

[2] Kenneth L. Gentry, *He Shall Have Dominion* (Institutes for Christian Economics, Tyler, TX, 1992), cover

do anything to impact the culture?" The fact is Christ intends to use the Church, by the power of the Holy Spirit, to win the world and put all His enemies under His feet *before* His return. The wind of God is at the back of the Church, not in her face.

How Did We Get Here?

You might be asking yourself, *"How is it that the church has received this doctrine so universally?"* One of the greatest problems we face in the contemporary church is our ignorance of history and lack of intelligent scholarship. I've heard Charles Capps say many times, *"The Bible is so simple you need help to misunderstand it."* The fact is, we have had a lot of help! Jesus said in Luke 6:40, *"A disciple is not above his teacher, but everyone who is perfectly trained will be like his teacher."*

The Church gets her doctrine from her preachers. Most of today's preacher learned in Bible college the eschatology of the denomination or group the which the school represents. Most of them are never taught comparative theology, comparing the various positions on a particular subject. For example, there are really only two theological positions on soteriology (the study of salvation): Calvinism and Arminianism. There are only four basic eschatological positions: amillennialism, classical premillennialism, dispensational premillennialism, and postmillennialism. Most schools teach their own position and remain silent (or make random criticisms) of the other positions they know little about. So when the students leave the classroom and enter the pulpit, they simply parrot the doctrine they have learned in school.

For example, I went to Rhema Bible Training Center in

Introduction

Tulsa, Oklahoma. I learned the theology and eschatology of the Word of Faith movement, which happens to be dispensational premillennialism. I do not question the motives of my teachers, they were sincere and dedicated. They were simply repeating what *they* had learned where they had been trained. I was not taught that there are four basic eschatological positions. It was only after fifteen years of pastoring (teaching my congregation dispensational premillennialism) that, by God's grace, I heard about the other positions, examined each of them in the light of scripture and *adjusted my eschatology!* In this book you will get a chance to see the other side of the story, as I did after fifteen years.

A Challenge To The Reader

I challenge you to examine the facts for yourself and come to your own conclusions after seeing all the evidence. You will see how thoroughly scriptural, simple and logical this teaching is and wonder why you did not see it before. You will also see that premillennial dispensationalism is scripturally indefensible. But you must have an open mind. May God give you the grace to receive new (really old) truth by which you can wage a good warfare!

CHAPTER 2

Darby & Company

And I saw an angel come down from heaven, having the key of the bottomless pit and a great chain in his hand. And he laid hold on the dragon, that old serpent, which is the Devil and Satan and bound him a **thousand years**, And cast him into the bottomless pit and shut him up and set a seal upon him, that he should deceive the nations no more, till the **thousand years** should be fulfilled: and after that he must be loosed a little season. And I saw thrones and they sat upon them and judgment was given unto them; and I saw the souls of them that were beheaded for the witness of Jesus and for the word of God and which had not worshiped the beast, neither his image, neither had received his mark upon their foreheads, or in their hands; and they lived and reigned with Christ a **thousand years**. But the rest of the dead

> lived not again until the **thousand years** were finished. This is the first resurrection. Blessed and holy is he that hath part in the first resurrection: on such the second death hath no power, but they shall be priests of God and of Christ and shall reign with him a **thousand years**. And when the **thousand years** are expired, Satan shall be loosed out of his prison," (Rev 20:1-7) (Emphasis added)

Before considering the legacy of John Nelson Darby it is important to put it into the historical perspective of the other eschatological positions. While this chapter may seem somewhat tedious in its detail, it is necessary to get a clear perspective of Darby's system compared with the other historical positions. I promise the following chapters will be a much easier read!

As we have seen, there are only four major eschatological schemes: amillennialism, classical premillennialism, dispensational premillennialism, and postmillennialism. The root word, *millennial*, depending on the scheme, refers to, either a literal or a symbolic one thousand year reign of Christ mentioned in Revelation, chapter twenty. The time would be one of a golden age on Earth of righteousness and justice coupled with the extinction, or at least a great diminishing of, evil. The prefixes, *"a," "pre,"* and *"post"* refer to the time relative to the millennium when Christ will physically return to Earth.

Amillennialism

Therefore, the <u>a</u>millennial scheme expects no Millennium or Golden Age of gospel expansion. The *"thousand years"* is seen to be symbolic, representing a long, unspecified period of time. During that time *the reign of Christ is from Heaven and only extends to the Church and the individual believer, not all the inhabitants of the Earth.* Thus they expect victory and defeat, success and failure, good and evil, to coexist on Earth in varying degrees until Christ comes with rewards and judgments at the end of time. This position was held by Polycarp (A.D. 69-105), Ignatius (about A.D. 150) and currently by Roman Catholics, some evangelicals and much of mainline, denominational Protestantism.[1]

Classical Premillennialism

George Eldon Ladd, a leading advocate of this system describes it as follows:

> *... Premillennialism is the doctrine stating that after the Second Coming of Christ, he will reign for a thousand years over the earth before the final consummation of God's redemptive purpose in the new heavens and the new earth of the Age to Come. This is the natural reading of Revelation 20:1-6.*
>
> *Revelation 19:11-16 pictures the Second Coming of Christ as a conqueror coming to destroy his enemies: the Antichrist, Satan and Death. Revelation 19:17-21 pictures first the destruction of Antichrist and the hosts which have supported him in opposition to the kingdom of God. Revelation 20 then relates the destruction of the evil power behind the Antichrist .... this occurs in 'two stages.*

---

[1] Jeffery L. Sheler, *The Christmas Covenant*, U.S. News & World Report, December 19, 1994, p.66

> *First, Satan is bound and incarcerated in 'the bottomless pit' (Rev. 20: 1) for a thousand years.... At this time occurs the 'first resurrection' (Rev. 20:5) of saints who share Christ's rule over the earth for the thousand years. After this Satan is loosed from his bonds and in spite of the fact that Christ has reigned over the earth for a thousand years, he finds the hearts of unregenerated men still ready to rebel against God. The final eschatological war follows when the devil is thrown into the lake of fire and brimstone. Then occurs a second resurrection of those who had not been raised before the millennium....*
>
> **The gospel is not to conquer the world and subdue all nations to itself.** *Hatred, conflict and war will continue to characterize the age until the coming of the Son of Man.... Evil will mark the course of the age.*[2] (Emphasis added)

This system of end-time thought should not be confused with the current eschatological rage, *dispensational* premillennialism. The key difference is that classical premillennialism *has always taught that the Church* <u>would</u> *go through the Great Tribulation prior to Christ's physical return*. This will be *followed* by Christ's physical return and literal thousand year reign on Earth, at the end of which time Christ will judge the Earth. While the proponents in the Early Church included Justin Martyr (100-165), Irenaeus (130-

---

[2] George E. Ladd, *Historic Premillennialism, Meaning of the Millennium*, p.17

202) and Tertullian (160-220), few hold this view today.

Postmillennialism

The position held overwhelmingly by the historic Christian church is the *post*millennial system, with the expected return of Christ only after the Great Commission is fulfilled and all of Christ's enemies are put under His feet by the Holy Spirit empowered Church. The list of adherents to this eschatological system begins with the Church Fathers, continues through the Early Church, the Reformation, the Pilgrims, Puritans, Calvinists and most of the Revivalists of the First and Second Great Awakening. The list is long and distinguished:

> *In the ancient church: Eusebius (*A.D. *260-340), Athanasius (*A.D. *296-372) and Augustine (*A.D. *354-430). In the modern church: J. A. Alexander, O. T. Allis, Greg Bahnsen, Albert Barnes, David Brown, John Calvin, Roderick Campbell, Robert L. Dabney, John Jefferson Davis, Jonathan Edwards, Matthew Henry, A. A. Hodge, Charles Hodge, Erroll Hulse, Francis Nigel Lee, Marcellus Kik, J. Gresham Machen, George C. Miladin, Iain Murray, John Murray, Gary North, John Owen, R. J. Rushdoony, Steve Schlissel W. G. T. Shedd, Norman Shepherd, Augustus H. Strong, J. H. Thornwell, Richard C. Trench, B. B. Warfield and many of the Puritans.*[3]

The system is comprehensively summed up by Gentry:

---

[3] Kenneth L. Gentry, *He Shall Have Dominion* (Institute for Christian Economics, Tyler, TX, 1992), p.91

First, postmillennialism is that system of eschatology which understands the Messianic kingdom to have been founded upon the earth during the earthly ministry and through the redemptive labors of the Lord Jesus Christ. This establishment of the "kingdom of heaven" was in fulfillment of Old Testament prophetic expectation...

Second, the fundamental nature of that kingdom is essentially redemptive and spiritual rather than political and corporeal.... **Christ rules His kingdom spiritually in and through His people in the world (representation), as well as by His universal providence.**

Third, **His kingdom will exercise a transformational sociocultural influence in history.** *This will occur as more and more people are converted to Christ, not by a minority revolt and seizure of political power.* **The essential distinctive of postmillennialism is its scripturally derived, sure expectation of gospel prosperity for the church during the present age.**

Fourth, **postmillennialism, thus, expects the gradual, developmental expansion of the kingdom of Christ in time and on earth....Christ's personal presence on earth is not needed for the expansion of His kingdom.**

Fifth, postmillennialism confidently anticipates a time in earth's history (continuous with the pre-

*sent) in which the very gospel already operative in the world will have won the victory throughout the earth in fulfillment of the Great Commission. The thing that distinguishes the biblical postmillennialist, then, from amillennialists and premillennialists is **his belief that the Scripture teaches the success of the great commission in this age of the church**. During that time the overwhelming majority of men and nations will be Christianized, righteousness will abound, wars will cease and prosperity and safety will flourish.*[4] (Emphasis added)

One important point which needs to be made about this system is that it views the thousand year reign of Christ to be a symbolic, rather than literal, one thousand years. Since the Book of Revelation is the only place the *"thousand years"* is mentioned and Revelation is largely symbolic in its content, this is a exegetically sound assumption. In fact to interpret it literally as the dispensationalists do, is actually unsound exegesis.

Consider this definition: *"Thousand—A number often used as a metaphor for a large, indefinite number of people, things or length of time. Deut. 1:11; 7:9; 32:30; Josh. 23:10; Job 9:3; 33:23; Ps.50:10; 84:10; 90A 91:7; Ecc. 6:6; 7:28; Song. 4:4; 8:11,12; Isa. 30:17; 60:22; 2 Pet. 3:8; Rev. 20:2-7"*[5] For example, Psa. 50:10 says, *"For every beast of the forest is mine and the cattle upon a **thousand hills**."* Does God own

---

[4] Kenneth L. Gentry, *He Shall Have Dominion* (Institute for Christian Economics, Tyler, TX, 1992), p.70-71 (Emphasis added)

[5] W. Stuart Owen, *A Dictionary of Bible Symbols* (Grace Publications Trust, London, England, 1992), p.115

the cattle of only a thousand hills, or is the *"thousand"* referring to a large, indefinite number? Or, as in 1 Chron. 16:15, *"Be ye mindful always of his covenant; the word which he commanded to a **thousand generations;**"* is His word only to a thousand generations, or to all generations?

Instead of arbitrarily assuming that history will conclude after six thousand years, followed by a one thousand year Millennium, as the dispensationalists do, the postmillennialist expects history to continue possibly for many thousands of years. This does two things. First it removes the inordinate desire to set times and dates for Christ's return which Christ warned stringently against. Second, it accords with Christ's description of how the Kingdom of God, like leaven, would eventually, slowly, almost unseen, over a long period of time expand to fill the whole earth.

> *Another parable put he forth unto them, saying, The kingdom of heaven is like to a grain of mustard seed, which a man took and sowed in his field: Which indeed is the least of all seeds: but **when it is grown, it is the greatest among herbs** and becometh a tree, so that the birds of the air come and lodge in the branches thereof. Another parable spake he unto them; The kingdom of heaven is like unto leaven, which a woman took and hid in three measures of meal, **till the whole was leavened.*** (Matt. 13:31-33) (Emphasis added)

Darby & Dispensational Premillennialism

The currently popular eschatology is the system invented in the 1830s by John Nelson Darby, founder of the Plymouth Brethren. It has been embraced by almost all Baptist, Word of Faith, charismatic, independent and fundamental churches. Few, if any, of these groups are aware of its absence of *any* supporters in the Early Church, its *strong opponents* at the time of its origination, or the *many* (as we will describe in the following chapters) *scriptural contradictions* presented by this system of thought, or the *demoralizing effect* on gospel expansion when this philosophy is carried out to its logical conclusion.

Most of these adherents would be shocked (as I was) to find out there is *absolutely no question* that this system was introduced by J. N. Darby in the 1830s. It had *never been heard of* in the early, Roman, Eastern Orthodox, or Protestant church prior to Darby's introduction.

> *It is the premillennialist view, with its elaborate timetables and graphic end-of-the-world scenarios, that has captured the most attention in recent years and that now has become the focus of scholarly scrutiny. While there are differences of opinion within the tradition,* **the dominant view, called dispensationalism, has its root in the teachings of John Nelson Darby, a 19th-century Englishman and founder of the Plymouth Brethren.** *He taught that history is divided into seven ages, or dispensations, which will culminate in the final judgment and the end of the world. The dispensationalist scenario, popularized recently in evangelical writer Hal Lindsey's 1970 bestseller,* <u>The Late Great Planet Earth</u> *and by Dallas Theological Seminary Chancellor John Walvoord's* <u>Armageddon, Oil and the Middle East Crisis</u>, *is drawn largely from the Old Testament prophecy books of Ezekiel,*

Zechariah and Daniel and the enigmatic New Testament book of Revelation.[6] (Emphasis added)

The Elwell Evangelical Dictionary confirms both Darby's origination of the system and the major difference from all previous teaching:

Darby, John Nelson, (1800-1882). The most influential British leader of the separatist Plymouth Brethren movement (also known as Darbyites) and systematizer of dispensationalism. His ideas pervaded late nineteenth century millenarianism in England and America and became a prominent element in American fundamentalism.

He divided history into separate eras or dispensations, each of which contained a different order by which God worked out his redemptive plan. The age of the church, like all preceding periods, has ended in failure due to man's sinfulness. **Darby broke not only from previous millenarian teaching but from all of church history by asserting that Christ's second coming would occur in two stages. The first, an invisible "secret rapture" of true believers, could happen at any moment, ending the great "parenthesis" or church age which began when the Jews rejected Christ.** (Emphasis added)

Virtually every source indicates J. N. Darby to be the

---

[6] Jeffery L. Sheler, *The Christmas Covenant*, U.S. News & World Report, December 19, 1994, p.66 (Emphasis added)

source of dispensational premillennialism, with no precedent in history. The *Spirit Filled Life Bible* comments on this fact and also comments on the inconsistency of Pentecostals and charismatics accepting this scheme of interpretation:

> ***The dispensational interpretation is the most recent to appear in church history.*** *The "dispensational" scheme of redemptive history presupposes two different peoples of God throughout history—Israel and the church—and, therefore, two programs of prophecy. The seven letters to the seven churches are interpreted "prophetically" as an outline of a seven-stage church age. Revelation 4:1 is interpreted as the Rapture of the church, understood as the secret departure of all believers to heaven before "the great tribulation." The rest of the book is then seen as concerned exclusively with "the great tribulation" and the fate of Israel at the hands of the Antichrist. According to this view, Christ returns to destroy the Beast, to bind Satan and to introduce His thousand-year reign on Earth. Dispensationalists view this Millennium as the time when the Jewish theocracy, with the temple, the sacrificial system and the Law of Moses, is restored and the Old Testament prophecies concerning Israel's future political triumph over the Gentiles are literally-physically fulfilled.*
>
> *(Interestingly, many of Pentecostal/ Charismatic tradition interpret Revelation and Daniel from this dispensational view, even though* ***such an interpretive approach anywhere other than in prophetic***

> *scripture would dictate a denial of the present manifestation of the gifts of the Spirit.)*[7]

Even Darby himself was aware of the fact that his newfound "revelation" was contrary to all previous thought on this subject. His shocking commentary also reveals the negativity of his system versus the optimism of the previously universally accepted postmillenarian system. Here are Darby's own words:

> *What we are about to consider will tend to show that,* ***instead of permitting ourselves to hope for a continued progress of good, we must expect a progress of evil;*** *and that the hope of the earth being filled with the knowledge of the Lord before the exercise of His judgment and the consummation of this judgment on the earth, is delusive.*
>
> ***We are to expect evil,*** *until it becomes so flagrant that it will be necessary for the Lord to judge it...**I am afraid that many a cherished feeling, dear to the children of God, has been shocked this evening; I mean, their hope that the gospel will spread by itself over the whole earth during the actual dispensation.***[8] (Emphasis added)

David Bogue, a preacher of the era, expressed his sentiment concerning his strong reservations about the system:

---

[7] *Spirit Filled Life Bible*, (Thomas Nelson Publishers, 1991), p.1953 (Emphasis added)

[8] J. N. Darby in a lecture delivered in Geneva in 1840 on *Progress of Evil on the Earth*. (The Collected Writings of Y. N. Darby, Prophetic, Vol. 1), 471 and 483 (Emphasis added)

*How wise and pious men could ever suppose that the saints, whose souls are now in Heaven, should, after the resurrection of the body from the grave, descend to live on earth again; and that Jesus Christ should quit the throne of His glory above and descend and reign personally over them here below in distinguished splendor for a thousand years, may justly excite our astonishment since **it is in direct opposition to the whole tenor of the doctrinal parts of the sacred volume**. Such, however, have been the opinions of some great men. **Happy will it be if we take warning from their aberrations.***[9] (Emphasis added)

Who Puffed Darby?

In 1951 Billy Graham was an unknown evangelist with a limited ministry and reputation until William Randolph Hearst heard of him. Hearst issued his famous two word telegram, *"Puff Graham"* to his newspapers. The rest is history. The question you might have is, Who "puffed" Darby's doctrine and made this unknown figure (or at least his eschatological views) a household word?

The answer can be found in the people whom Darby influenced:

> *In 1909,* **Cyrus Ingerson Scofield** *(1843-1921) caused a considerable stir in the religious world when he boldly placed his comments on the page of the inspired text. After all, how could the com-*

---

[9] Iain H. Murray, *The Puritan Hope, Revival and the Interpretation of Prophecy* (Banner of Truth Trust, Edinburgh, England, 1971), p.187 (Emphasis added)

mon reader distinguish between the learned remarks of the editor and the words of holy writ? But the study Bible that bore his name soon became the most popular study Bible among conservative believers throughout the English-speaking world.

So great was the response that Oxford University Press revised and republished it in 1917, 1937, 1945, and 1967.

Despite the decided dispensational slant of the editor and negative view of charismata, **no study Bible in history has so shaped the theology of the last three generations of Bible students-including charismatics—as the Scofield Reference Bible.**

How much of Scofield's theology was transferred to the millions of believers who came to love and trust his study Bible? Though charismatics discovered Scofield's denial of the Holy Spirit's supernatural power for modern times unacceptable (he believed the gifts and miracles ceased with the early Church), they adopted his dispensational structure of theology. **Despite the fact that this dispensationalism was superimposed on the pages of Scripture, and directly contradicted emerging Pentecostal theology, charismatics using the Bible tended to accept Scofield's theological system.**

*P. H. Alexander states in the Dictionary of Pentecostal and Charismatic Movements that the impact of the Scofield Reference Bible on the Pentecostal and charismatic movements "was early and direct in this country and can scarcely be understated . . . **Some charismatics, as was often the case with theological issues, accepted dispensationalism by default as part of the whole theological package accompanying the baptism of the Holy Spirit.**[10]* (Emphasis added)

Iain Murray, in his classic *The Puritan Hope* comments:

*Among the many who absorbed Darby's teaching was Henry Moorhouse, an evangelist among the Brethren, who, in turn, influenced **D. L. Moody**. Before the end of the nineteenth century Moody was probably the most esteemed evangelical figure on both sides of the Atlantic and the Bible College named after him at Chicago became a seminary of ardent premillennial belief. The impact of Darby on another American, **C. I. Scofield**, was still more momentous, for **Scofield's notes made his master's teaching on prophecy an integral part of the Reference Bible first published in 1909 and thereafter wedded to Scofield's name**. Within fifty years approximately three million copies of the Scofield Reference Bible were printed in America, a proportionate number were issued by the Oxford University Press in Britain and **the volume had*

---

[10] Dan Hedges, *Finding Your Way Through The Study Bible Maze*, (ORUEF Newsletter, Nov. 2000), p.5 (Emphasis added)

vast influence in making Darby's prophetical beliefs the norm for evangelicals in the English-speaking world.[11] (Emphasis added)

The influence of Moody and Scofield gave credibility to Darby and his doctrine. Soon the Scofield Bible and its notes became the rage in evangelical and fundamental circles, and as a matter of course invaded the Bible Colleges, like Moody, Dallas Theological Seminary and many others. It became the accepted eschatology of fundamentalism; and later, of the Charismatic Movement.

It is notable that recently, given dispensationalism's many failed prophecies predicting the time of the Rapture[12] almost all of these institutions have begun to question dispensational premillennialism as a tenet of faith:

But now some conservative evangelical scholars are beginning to challenge them as well. Professors at such bastions of premillennialism as Dallas Theological Seminary, Moody Bible Institute in Chicago and Wheaton College in Wheaton, Ill., recently have raised strong objections to the literal interpretation of some apocalyptic texts and to the intense search for "signs of the times" in current events.

In their forthcoming book, <u>Doomsday Delusions</u>,

---

[11] Ibid., p.198 (Emphasis added)
[12] Beginning with William Miller (1844), Darby, *"The Lord will unquestionably return in 1867,"* Billy Graham in 1950, *"Two years and its going to be all over,"* Whisenant, *88 Reasons the Lord Will Return in 1988*, Harold Camping, 1994; and many others.

> *Moody Professors C. Marvin Pate and Calvin B. Haines Jr. argue that **premillennial doomsday preachers often "misinterpret and misapply" biblical prophecies by ignoring their historical context.***
>
> *At Wheaton College, growing faculty disaffection with the school's rigid adherence to premillennialist doctrine prompted school officials recently **to drop the view from its doctrinal statement**. "It's just not an essential part of the Christian faith," explains New Testament Prof. Alan Johnson. Even at Jerry Falwell's fundamentalist Liberty University in Lynchburg, Va., New Testament Prof. D. Brent Sandy challenges the notion that details of future events can be extracted from the Bible.*[13]
>
> (Emphasis added)

So, as you can see, Darby's doctrine may be in vogue now, but winds of change are beginning to blow and with good reason. I cannot think of any accepted doctrine of the orthodox church that doesn't have its roots in the Early Church along with repeated emphasis through history. While the fact that Darby's scheme has no precedent in the historical Church does not necessarily make it errant, it certainly gives one reason to examine its accuracy in light of God's own word.

That is what we will consider in the succeeding chapters.

---

[13] Jeffery L. Sheler, *The Christmas Covenant,* U.S. News & World Report, December 19, 1994, p.67, 68, 71 (Emphasis added)

CHAPTER 3

The Mysterious Gap

*Seventy weeks are determined **upon thy people and upon thy holy city**, to finish the transgression and to make an end of sins and to make reconciliation for iniquity and to bring in everlasting righteousness and to seal up the vision and prophecy and to anoint the most Holy. Know therefore and understand, that from the going forth of the commandment to restore and to build Jerusalem unto the Messiah the Prince shall be **seven weeks and threescore and two weeks**: the street shall be built again and the wall, even in troublous times.* **(DARBY'S MYSTERIOUS GAP)** *And after threescore and two weeks shall Messiah be cut off, but not for himself. And the people of the prince that shall come shall destroy the city and the sanctuary; and the end thereof shall be with a flood and unto the end of the war desolations are deter-*

*mined. And he shall confirm the covenant with many for **one week**: and in the **midst of the week** he shall cause the sacrifice and the oblation to cease and for the overspreading of abominations he shall make it **desolate**, even until the **consummation** and that determined shall be poured upon **the desolate**.* Daniel 9:24-27 (Emphasis added)

Daniel's Seventy Weeks

All biblical prophecy hinges on the interpretation of Daniel's Seventy Weeks found in Daniel, chapter nine. Daniel received this prophecy in about 538 B.C. It gives a specific chronological timetable of 490 years[1] until the end of God's exclusive dealings with the Jews and Jerusalem (*"Seventy weeks are determined upon thy people [Jews] and upon thy holy city [Jerusalem]"*). The weekly segments of time describe historical events that were to take place.

Seven weeks (49 years) would begin with a decree to rebuild Jerusalem (*"from the going forth of the commandment to restore and to build Jerusalem"*). This event occurred in 457 B.C. with the decree by Artaxerxes to rebuild the city of Jerusalem.

"Know therefore and understand, that from the going forth of the commandment to restore and to build Jerusalem unto the Messiah the Prince shall be seven weeks and threescore and two weeks:" Following the completion of construction, after another sixty-two weeks (434 years) the Messiah (Jesus) would begin His ministry (27 A.D.). The Jews understood this prophecy would have a literal fulfillment in time and as a result they were anticipating Messiah's

---

[1] This universally accepted "one day equals one year" scheme of interpretation is taken from Ezek. 4:4-6

The Mysterious Gap

birth around the time of Augustus's census.[2]

"And after threescore and two weeks shall Messiah be cut off, but not for himself...And he shall confirm the covenant with many for one week: and in the midst of the week he shall cause the sacrifice and the oblation to cease". The final one week (7 years) would include Messiah's 3½ year earthly ministry, His death and the end of the sacrificial system.[3]

"And the people of the prince that shall come shall destroy the city and the sanctuary; and the end thereof shall be with a flood and unto the end of the war desolations are determined...and for the overspreading of abominations he shall make it desolate, even until the consummation and that determined shall be poured upon the desolate." After the Crucifixion, for the last 3½ years of the seventieth week, Christ continued His covenant to preach to the Jews only, through His disciples. They later, (in Acts 8), were scattered by persecution and went to the Samaritans and Gentiles, but only after the seven-year exclusively Jewish covenant was fulfilled. The utter and devastating judgment of the Jews for their rejection of their Messiah commenced and was later consummated, with the utter destruction of Jerusalem, the Temple and the dispersion of the Jews.[4]

The three segments of the seventy week period, with each

---

[2] This included Herod, the Magi and all Jerusalem (Matt. 2:1-3), Simeon (Luke 2:25-35) and Anna the Prophetess (Luke 2:36-36)

[3] At the moment of Jesus' death with His comment, *"It is finished..."* there was a great earthquake and the curtain dividing the Holy Place from the Most Holy Place was torn in two from top to bottom. Messiah was "cut off" at the exact middle of the seventieth week! No sacrifices were ever again offered in the Temple until its destruction in 70 A.D.

[4] The desolation foretold in Daniel 9:26-27 was referred to by Jesus in Matt. 23:38 and Luke 21:20-24 and fulfilled in amazing detail in 70 A.D.

day representative of one year, adds up to 490 years (7 + 62 + 1 = 70). It *was* historically fulfilled in consecutive order precisely as Daniel said it would be.

Darby's Parenthesis

John Nelson Darby's system rests its full weight on his novel method of dividing the Seventy Weeks. What Darby did was divide or "break" the Seventy Weeks in a way no one else had ever thought of. His system proposed that there was a "gap" or "historical parenthesis" between the 69th and 70th weeks, which was not foreseen by any of the Old Testament prophets. He called it, "the Church Age," or "Age of Mystery" because of the apparent "blind spot" of the prophets.

According to Darby the Jewish time clock stopped with the death of Messiah at the end of the 69th Week. The intervening period of time would be the "Church Age," the length of time between Pentecost and the "Secret Rapture" of the Church (which has now extended to almost 2000 years), in which God would deal primarily with the Gentiles. Only when the Church had been "raptured out," would the Jewish time clock again begin ticking out the yet unfulfilled 70th Week.

The 70th Week would be the time of the Tribulation, during which the Antichrist would rise to rule the world and God would begin to pour out the fierce judgments mentioned in the Revelation. At the end of the Tribulation Christ would physically return, crush the forces of the Antichrist and establish a physical reign over earth's inhabitants (including mortal men, surviving Tribulation saints and resurrected believers of the previous ages) and bind Satan.

The Gap Disappears

It cannot be stated strongly enough that **Darby's whole system is dependent on the existence of this "gap" or "parenthesis."** If there is no "gap" then Darby's whole system of interpretation falls. And as will be simply and conclusively proved, there is no support for this "gap" in the text, the context, or anywhere else in scripture!

> *And **AFTER** threescore and two weeks shall Messiah be cut off, but not for himself. And the people of the prince that shall come shall destroy the city and the sanctuary; and the end thereof shall be with a flood and unto the end of the war desolations are determined. And he shall confirm the covenant with many for **one week**: and in the **midst of the week** he shall cause the sacrifice and the oblation to cease and for the overspreading of abominations he shall make it **desolate**, even until the **consummation** and that determined shall be poured upon **the desolate**.* Daniel 9:26-27 (Emphasis added)

First, if language has any meaning at all, the Messiah's ministry occurred in Daniel's 70th Week. Doesn't 70 follow after 69? And that is what the scripture plainly says, *"And AFTER threescore and two weeks* (the 7 weeks plus the 62 weeks) *shall Messiah be cut off..."* Jesus Christ, the Messiah, was crucified (*"cut off"*) **after the 69th Week, in the 70th Week, just as the scripture declares!**

There is no question that Jesus' earthly ministry (the time after His baptism) lasted for 3½ years until He was crucified (cut off or killed). It was during Daniel's 70th Week. The next verse refers to the 70th Week, *"...one week...midst of the week...."* (7+62+1). Jesus, the Messiah, was killed in the middle of the 70th week, exactly as predicted. As we have seen, at the exact time He died, the Temple sacrificial system ended—again, just as predicted!

> *...and for the overspreading of abominations he shall make it **desolate**, even until the **consummation** and that determined shall be poured upon **the desolate**."*(Emphasis added)

Daniel's last week (seven years) included the 3½ years of Jesus' preaching exclusively to the Jews, followed by His disciples fulfilling the seven year covenant by also preaching to Jews alone. After this time began the ***desolation*** of the Jews and Jerusalem in judgment for their rejection of Christ. The ***consummation*** took place in 70 A.D. with the destruction of Jerusalem and the Temple (with every stone literally pried loose by the Romans who were looking for gold melted between the stones) and the dispersion of the Jews, the ***generational judgment predicted exactly by Jesus:***

> *Wherefore ye be witnesses unto yourselves, that ye are the children of them which killed the prophets. Fill ye up then the measure of your fathers. Ye serpents, ye **generation** of vipers, how can ye escape the damnation of hell? Wherefore, behold, I send unto you prophets and wise men and scribes: and some of them ye shall kill and crucify; and some of them shall ye scourge in your synagogues and persecute them from city to city: **That upon you may come all the righteous blood shed upon the***

> ***earth**, from the blood of righteous Abel unto the blood of Zacharias son of Barachias, whom ye slew between the temple and the altar. **Verily I say unto you, All these things shall come upon this generation.** O Jerusalem, Jerusalem, thou that killest the prophets and stonest them which are sent unto thee, how often would I have gathered thy children together, even as a hen gathereth her chickens under her wings and ye would not! Behold, your house is left unto you **desolate**. For I say unto you, Ye shall not see me henceforth, till ye shall say, Blessed is he that cometh in the name of the Lord. And Jesus went out and departed from the temple: and his disciples came to him for to shew him the buildings of the temple. And Jesus said unto them, See ye not all these things? **verily I say unto you, There shall not be left here one stone upon another, that shall not be thrown down**.* Matthew 23:31-24:2 (Emphasis added)

Luke's gospel also refers to this utter desolation which actually was fulfilled in minute detail in 70 A.D.:

> *And when **ye shall see Jerusalem compassed with armies**, then know that the **desolation** thereof is nigh. Then let them which are in Judaea flee to the mountains; and let them which are in the midst of it depart out; and let not them that are in the countries enter thereinto. **For these be the days of vengeance, that all things which are written may be fulfilled.** But woe unto them that are with child and to them that give suck, in those days! **for there*

*shall be great distress in the land and wrath upon this people. And they shall fall by the edge of the sword and shall be **led away captive into all nations: and Jerusalem shall be trodden down of the Gentiles**, until the times of the Gentiles be fulfilled.* Luke 21:20-24 (Emphasis added)

Could it be any more plain! Daniel's 70th Week followed consecutively after the 69th Week, with every detail supported by verified historical events. The 70th Week of Daniel is not some date yet in the future, **it has already occurred!**

Remember Charles Capps, *"The Bible is so simple you need help to misunderstand it."* Darby and his adherents have given us plenty of help!

Daniel's Perspective of Time

One last point on this subject. We have mentioned the fact that the "gap" theory violates not only the text, but the context in which it was written. Daniel lived during the seventy-year Babylonian Captivity. The Jews were displaced in judgment for 490 years of Sabbath Day violations, one year for every seven of disobedience, or seventy years. *"And this whole land shall be a **desolation** and an astonishment; and these nations shall serve the king of Babylon **seventy years**. And it shall come to pass, when seventy years are accomplished, that I will punish the king of Babylon and that nation, saith the Lord, for their iniquity and the land of the Chaldeans and will make it **perpetual desolations**."* Jeremiah 25:11-12 (Emphasis added)

Daniel was well aware of this fact: *"In the first year of his reign I Daniel understood by books **the number of the years**, whereof the word of the Lord came to Jeremiah the* *prophet, that he would accomplish **seventy years** in the **desolations of Jerusalem**.*" (Daniel 9:2) (Emphasis added) What Daniel also knew was that the seventy years of captivity were to be consecutive. The 70th year would follow immediately after the 69th year. It was in this historical context that he wrote his prophecy and expected its fulfillment to take place, not with a "gap" between years, but in chronological and consecutive order.

This chapter alone is sufficient to disprove dispensational eschatology, but there are many more proofs of the error of this system. In the next chapter we will observe another glaring error, which also, by itself, is capable of derailing the dispensational train. That error is the assumption by Darby and other dispensationalists, that there will be another world-dominating kingdom, ruled by the Antichrist prior to Christ's physical return. Daniel was absolutely clear that there would be no government or ruler that would rule the earth after Rome. The Fifth Kingdom predicted by Daniel, beginning during the time of Rome, would conquer all other kingdoms until Christ returned. That Kingdom was the Kingdom of God!

CHAPTER 4

The Fifth Kingdom

This is the dream; and we will tell the interpretation thereof before the king. **Thou, O king, art a king of kings**: *for the God of heaven hath given thee a kingdom, power and strength and glory. And wheresoever the children of men dwell, the beasts of the field and the fowls of the heaven hath he given into thine hand and hath made thee ruler over them all.* **Thou art this head of gold**. *And after thee shall arise* **another kingdom** *inferior to thee and* **another third kingdom** *of brass, which shall bear rule over all the earth. And* **the fourth kingdom shall be strong as iron**: *forasmuch as iron breaketh in pieces and subdueth all things: and as iron that breaketh all these, shall it break in pieces and bruise. And whereas thou sawest the feet and toes, part of potters' clay and part of iron,* **the kingdom shall be divided**; *but there shall be in* *it of the strength of the iron, forasmuch as thou sawest the iron mixed with miry clay. And as the toes of the feet were part of iron and part of clay, so the kingdom shall be partly strong and partly broken. And whereas thou sawest iron mixed with miry clay, they shall mingle themselves with the seed of men: but they shall not cleave one to another, even as iron is not mixed with clay. And **<u>in the days of these kings</u> shall the God of heaven set up a kingdom, which shall never be destroyed: and the kingdom shall not be left to other people, but it shall break in pieces and consume all these kingdoms and it shall stand for ever.*** Daniel 2:36-44 (Emphasis added)

As mentioned previously, I taught the premil system for fifteen years. I know it very well and so am very familiar with its talking points. One of those is that after the Rapture of the Church, an Antichrist will arise to rule the world out of a revived, ten nation, Roman Empire. Much talk in recent years has revolved around the European Common Market as being the place out of which the Antichrist will appear. There is only one problem with this scenario—the word of God absolutely forbids it!

Daniel's Interpretation

The prophecy above is Daniel's interpretation of a dream given to Nebuchadnezzar, the King of Babylon. There are five world-dominating kingdoms mentioned. There is absolutely no problem in identifying these kingdoms with the perspective of recorded history.

The Fifth Kingdom

Thou, O king, art a king of kings*: for the God of heaven hath given thee a kingdom, power and strength and glory. And wheresoever the children of men dwell, the beasts of the field and the fowls of the heaven hath he given into thine hand and hath made thee ruler over them all.* ***Thou art this head of gold.***

Nebuchadnezzar was the ruler of Babylon and as any world history textbook will tell you, Babylon was the third kingdom[1] (for the purpose of this prophecy it was the first, see footnote 1) to rule the near-eastern world, from 741 to 538 B.C. Daniel lived as a captive in the last days of this kingdom, which was taken from Nebuchadnezzar's son, Belshazzar as recorded in Daniel 5:30-31:

In that night was Belshazzar the king of the Chaldeans slain. And Darius the Median took the kingdom, being about threescore and two years old.

And after thee shall arise **another kingdom** *inferior to thee....* The second kingdom to rule the world was Medo-Persia, from 538 to 336 B.C. As predicted and historically fulfilled, it never achieved the greatness of Babylon.

"*...and* **another third kingdom** *of brass, which shall bear rule over all the earth.*" Again, with the aid of history, identifying this kingdom is no problem either, it was the kingdom of Greece which ruled the known world from 336 to 62 B.C. Keep in mind this prophecy in Daniel chapter two is

---

[1] The first two were Assyria and Egypt. They were not mentioned here because they were already past and this prophecy describes the remaining kingdoms that would rule the world.

reaching hundreds of years into the future; but we have the perspective of historical hindsight.

*And **the fourth kingdom shall be strong as iron**: forasmuch as iron breaketh in pieces and subdueth all things: and as iron that breaketh all these, shall it break in pieces and bruise. And whereas thou sawest the feet and toes, part of potters' clay and part of iron, **the kingdom shall be divided**.* This kingdom too is easily identified, it was the kingdom of Rome which existed as a unified kingdom from 62 B.C. to 313 A.D., when, just as predicted by Daniel almost one thousand years earlier, **it was divided** and continued as such until 476 A.D. in the west, and until 1450 A.D. in the east.

The Fifth Kingdom

Now things begin to get very interesting! Notice what Daniel predicted would happen next. *And **in the days of these kings** shall the God of heaven set up a kingdom, **which shall never be destroyed**: and the kingdom shall not be left to other people, but it shall break in pieces and consume all these kingdoms **and it shall stand for ever**.* The kings of the Roman empire were called Caesars. In the days of Rome, the God of Heaven was going to initiate a Fifth Kingdom that would eventually rule over all the other kingdoms of the world. If God was going to set up a Kingdom, what do you think it might be called? How about "the Kingdom of God!"

Did this actually happen? Absolutely! Jesus, the Messiah, came into the earth during the Roman Empire at the time of the Caesars. With His Ascension He took His place in Heaven and began His reign over the earth. Scripture is unmistakably clear on the fact that Jesus is now reigning, not that He will reign after He comes physically. Consider 1 Cor. 15:25, *"**For he must reign, till** he hath put all enemies under his feet."* and

Rev. 1:4-5 *"John to the seven churches which are in Asia: Grace be unto you and peace, from him which is and which was and which is to come; and from the seven Spirits which are before his throne; And from **Jesus Christ**, who is the faithful witness and the first begotten of the dead and **the ruler over the kings of the earth**...." (Emphasis added)*

Jesus' millennial (remember, the thousand years was symbolic of a long, unspecified period of time) reign began with the Ascension, continues today and will do so until all of Christ's enemies are progressively defeated by the Spirit-empowered Church.

Jesus said the Kingdom would not be a visible (like a political or national kingdom), would expand slowly (like leaven, until the whole was leavened), but become great and expansive (like a mustard seed becoming a tree). Eventually, in the latter days, it would fill the earth. Isaiah 2:1-2

> *The word that Isaiah the son of Amoz saw concerning Judah and Jerusalem. And it shall come to pass in the latter days, that the **mountain**[2] **of the LORD's house** shall be established **in the top of the mountains** and shall be exalted above the hills; and **all nations shall flow unto it.** (Emphasis added)*

Or do you remember the great Messianic prophecy in Isaiah 9:6-7,

> *For unto us a child is born, unto us a son is given: and **the government shall be upon his shoulder:***

---

[2] Mountain: a metaphor for a king, a government or a nation and its power. W. Stuart Owen, *A Dictionary of Bible Symbols* (Grace Publications Trust, London, England, 1992), p.71

and his name shall be called Wonderful, Counselor, The mighty God, The everlasting Father, The Prince of Peace. ***Of the <u>increase of his government</u> and peace there shall be no end***, *upon the throne of David and upon his kingdom, to order it and to establish it with judgment and with justice **from henceforth even for ever**. The zeal of the* LORD *of hosts will perform this.* (Emphasis added)

The Dispensational Problem

Daniel chapters two and chapter seven (which repeats to Belshazzar the same scenario as chapter two) present an insurmountable obstacle to the dispensationalist because they absolutely forbid any other world-dominating kingdom (except the Kingdom of God) after Rome.

> Daniel 2:34-35 *Thou sawest till that a stone was cut out without hands* [the Kingdom of God], *which smote the image upon his feet that were of iron and clay (*Rome*) and brake them to pieces. Then was the iron, the clay, the brass, the silver and the gold, broken to pieces together and became like the chaff of the summer threshing floors; and **the wind carried them away, so that <u>no trace of them was found</u>**: and the stone* [the Kingdom of God] *that smote the image became a great mountain and filled the whole earth.*

The Roman Empire will not live again to provide a platform for the Antichrist to rule because God's word says it was *crushed* and *no trace of it would ever be found again!* This is just another fact, even if taken alone, without all the

The Fifth Kingdom

other proofs, which is fatal to dispensationalism. **There will never be another political kingdom (Rome or any other) that will rule the world because God had said there would only be the four earthly kingdoms** (which have come and gone) and the Kingdom of God, which is now growing slowly in the earth and will continue until it fills the earth! Here is a chart which shows what we have discussed about history and the future.

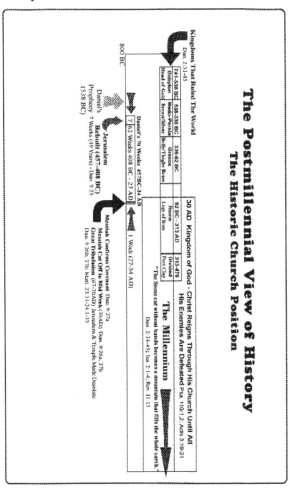

Think about it! Between 741 B.C. and 476 A.D., a period of 1217 years, there were four world kingdoms. Since 476 A.D. to the present, a period of 1525 years, there has not been even one more visible world kingdom. Why? Because God declared six hundred years before Christ what the times of nations would be. And right now Jesus is reigning from Heaven over His progressively expanding Kingdom (*Of the increase of his government and peace there shall be no end....* Isa. 9:7) God is and always has been in control. Glory to God!

Darby and his followers did get one thing right. The Antichrist did ascend from the Roman Empire (but that subject is for another chapter). But that was *in recorded history,* not the future.

CHAPTER 5

How Many Resurrections?

1 Cor. 15:22-26

> *For as in Adam all die, even so in Christ shall all be made alive. But every man in his own order: Christ the first fruits;* ***afterward they that are Christ's at his coming.*** *Then cometh the end, when he shall have delivered up the kingdom to God, even the Father; when he shall have put down all rule and all authority and power. For he must reign, till he hath put all enemies under his feet. The last enemy that shall be destroyed is death.* (Emphasis added)

1 Cor. 15:50-52

> *Now this I say, brethren, that flesh and blood cannot inherit the kingdom of God; neither doth corruption inherit incorruption. Behold, I shew you a mystery; We shall not all sleep, but we shall all be*

*changed, In a moment, in the twinkling of an eye, at **the last trump**: for the trumpet shall sound and the dead shall be raised incorruptible and we shall be changed.* (Emphasis added)

The hallmark of the premillennial system is the Rapture of the Church. The time when Christ returns in the clouds (invisible to sinners) and "catches away" the Church prior to the beginning of the seven year Tribulation, the *physical* return of Christ to rule the earth and finally the judgment. Common scenarios have planes crashing because the pilot is "raptured," men returning home to find their families gone and driver-less cars careening off of expressways. Again, there is only one problem. It is totally in opposition to scripture and the historical understanding of the Church.

Perhaps I should have said "raptures," since almost all who teach this system teach that there are multiple raptures. When I learned this system I was taught there would be seven "raptures; " Enoch, Elijah, Jesus, the Church, the 144,000 Jewish evangelists and finally the Two Witnesses. Unfortunately, this contradicts the Apostle Paul's teaching that at the same time as the Rapture will come the resurrection of the dead, *"...and the dead shall be raised incorruptible and we shall be changed."* (1 Cor. 15:52)

Only One Resurrection

The problem with this idea is that the overwhelming and plain teaching of scripture is that there will be **only one general resurrection** at the end of time. *But every man in his own order: Christ the first fruits;* ***afterward they that are***

How Many Resurrections?

Christ's at his coming. Then cometh the end, *when he shall have delivered up the kingdom to God, even the Father; when he shall have put down all rule and all authority and power. For he must reign, till he hath put all enemies under his feet.* ***The last enemy that shall be destroyed is death.*** (Emphasis added)

When Christ returns at the *"last trump"* it will be just that, the end. And with His return, the last enemy that has not been vanquished, death will be destroyed. That could not possibly be the case with the dispensational position, which teaches that God is going to massacre most of the inhabitants of the earth during the Tribulation.

Scripture, even from early times, is abundantly clear on the fact that there will be only one general resurrection (rapture). It will occur while one generation of people is alive on the earth. Job, for example, declares his certainty of a final resurrection:

Job 14:7-14

> *For there is hope of a tree, if it be cut down, that it will sprout again and that the tender branch thereof will not cease. Though the root thereof wax old in the earth and the stock thereof die in the ground; Yet through the scent of water it will bud and bring forth boughs like a plant. But man dieth and wasteth away: yea, man giveth up the ghost and where is he? As the waters fail from the sea and the flood decayeth and drieth up:* ***So man lieth down and riseth not: till the heavens be no more, they shall not awake, nor be raised out of their sleep.*** *Oh that thou wouldest hide me in the*

grave, that thou wouldest keep me secret, until thy wrath be past, that thou wouldest appoint me a set time and remember me! If a man die, shall he live again? **all the days of my appointed time will I wait, till my change come.** (Emphasis added)

Christ and His followers also taught **one general resurrection**:

John 5:28-29

Marvel not at this: for the hour is coming, in the which **all that are in the graves** *shall hear his voice,* **And shall come forth**; *they that have done good, unto the* **resurrection of life**; *and they that have done evil, unto the* **resurrection of damnation**. (Emphasis added)

John 6:39-40

And this is the Father's will which hath sent me, that of all which he hath given me I should lose nothing, but should **raise it up again at the last day**. *And this is the will of him that sent me, that* **every one** *which seeth the Son and believeth on him, may have everlasting life: and* **I will raise him up at the last day**. (Emphasis added)

John 6:44

No man can come to me, except the Father which hath sent me draw him: and **I will raise him up at** *the last day.* (Emphasis added)

John 6:53-54

*Then Jesus said unto them, Verily, verily, I say unto you, Except ye eat the flesh of the Son of man and drink his blood, ye have no life in you. Whoso eateth my flesh and drinketh my blood, hath eternal life; and **I will raise him up at the last day**.* (Emphasis added)

John 11:23-24

*Jesus saith unto her, Thy brother shall rise again. Martha saith unto him, I know that he shall rise again **in the resurrection at the last day**.* (Emphasis added)

Paul, who wrote all of the famous "Rapture" scriptures, including those quoted above, also taught elsewhere there would be one general resurrection:

Acts 17:30-33

*And the times of this ignorance God winked at; but now commandeth all men every where to repent: Because **he hath appointed a day, in the which he will judge the world** in righteousness by that man whom he hath ordained; whereof he hath given assurance unto all men, in that he hath raised him from the dead. And when **they heard of the resurrection of the dead**, some mocked: and* *others said, We will hear thee again of this matter. So Paul departed from among them.* (Emphasis added)

Acts 24:14-15

But this I confess unto thee, that after the way which they call heresy, so worship I the God of my fathers, believing all things which are written in the law and in the prophets: ¹⁵*And have hope toward God, which they themselves also allow, that* **there shall be a resurrection of the dead, both of the just and unjust.** (Emphasis added)

Follow The Rules!

One cardinal rule of Biblical interpretation is that unclear portions of scripture must be interpreted in the light of clear passages on the same subject. We have seen multiple, unmistakable, plain references from multiple credible witness that there will be only one resurrection. It will be at *"the last trump"* and *"at the end."* It can't be any more clear! That is why David Bogue was so incredulous when he heard about the dispensational system. His words bear repeating:

How wise and pious men could ever suppose that the saints, whose souls are now in Heaven, should, after the resurrection of the body from the grave, descend to live on earth again; and that Jesus Christ should quit the throne of His glory above and descend and reign personally over them here below in distinguished splendor for a

> *thousand years, may justly excite our astonishment since **it is in direct opposition to the whole tenor of the doctrinal parts of the sacred volume.** Such, however, have been the opinions of some great men. **Happy will it be if we take warning from their aberrations.***[1] (Emphasis added)

What the Bible clearly teaches about the resurrection of the dead alone is sufficient to refute premillennialism beyond any reasonable doubt. If there is only one resurrection as the Bible teaches, the multiple rapture doctrine of dispensationalism is clearly and unquestionably false!

What The Fathers Said

Adding to the list of witnesses against Darby's system is the unified voice of the Church Fathers in the historic creeds of the Church. The creeds were written to guarantee doctrinal orthodoxy and prevent heresy and error. Each of them pointedly refers to a single, end of time, resurrection and judgment of the just and unjust:

> **The Apostles' Creed:** "...*[Jesus Christ] ascended into heaven and sitteth on the right hand of God the Father Almighty; From thence **He shall come to judge the quick and the dead...**"*

> **The Nicene Creed:** "...*He ascended into heaven and sitteth on the right hand of the Father; And **He shall come again** with glory **to judge both the quick and the dead;** Whose Kingdom **shall have***

---

[1] Iain H. Murray, *The Puritan Hope, Revival and the Interpretation of Prophecy* (Banner of Truth Trust, Edinburgh, England, 1971), p.187

no end..."

The Athanasian Creed: *"...He ascended into heaven; He sitteth on the right hand of the Father, God Almighty; from whence **He shall come to judge the quick and the dead. At whose coming all men shall rise again with their bodies and shall give an account of their own works.** And they that have done good shall go into life everlasting; and they that have done evil, into everlasting fire..."*

These creeds are still in use today in all of Christendom and are regarded as authoritative. The amazing fact is they are even used in some churches that have embraced dispensational eschatology, because they have not seen the conflict posed to the creeds by multiple raptures or resurrections! Hopefully, we will see this trend reversed.

CHAPTER 6

How Short Is Shortly?

Rev. 1:1-3

> *The Revelation of Jesus Christ, which God gave unto him, to shew unto his servants* ***things which must shortly come to pass****; and he sent and signified it by his angel unto his servant John:* ²*Who bare record of the word of God and of the testimony of Jesus Christ and of all things that he saw.* ³*Blessed is he that readeth and they that hear the words of this prophecy and keep those things which are written therein: for* ***the time is at hand****.*
> (Emphasis added)

Perhaps the most serious flaw of the dispensational system is its playing fast and loose with biblical time references. Scriptures are *pressed into* the system rather than allowing the scriptures to *determine* the system. Clear references to time are often ignored or misinterpreted if they do not "fit" into Darby's system.

A prime example of this "time warp" is the handling of the book of Revelation. According to Darby's system, Revelation is a book describing a yet future time (now almost two thousand years into the future) in which the Rapture (or raptures), the Tribulation, the rise and fall of the Antichrist, and the physical return of Christ occur. But unless Jesus was *very* confused, He expected the events He predicted would take place in a relatively short period of time (one generation, about forty years) and that they would be observed firsthand by the first readers of the book, which was written between 64-68 A.D.[1] His language was clear and unambiguous.

Shortly Means Soon

The first verses make plain the expected time frame for fulfillment, *"...to shew unto his servants **things which must shortly come to pass**;..Blessed is he that readeth and they that hear the words of this prophecy and keep those things which are written therein: for **the time is at hand**."* (Emphasis added) The New King James version translates it, *"the time is **near**..."* *"Shortly,"* *"at hand"* and *"near"* are terms which indicate something is going to happen soon, not two thousand years later.

Even the dispensationalists realize the importance of this

---

[1] This date is widely accepted and well documented. For a complete discussion of the reason for this date see Kenneth L. Gentry, *Before Jerusalem Fell, Dating the Book of Revelation* (Institute for Christian Economics, Tyler, TX, 1989)

use of language and attempt to explain this apparent contradiction. Jack Van Impe, whose entire ministry rests on the study of eschatology, writes in his self-published reference Bible,

> The term 'shortly' in the original means 'rapidity of action once there is a beginning.' This certainly pictures the present hour when signs pointing to His return are beginning to appear with alarming frequency.[2]

This explanation obliterates any normal use of the word "*shortly*" as well as the context using the phrase "*at hand.*" If I'm going to meet you at a restaurant and tell you I'll be there "shortly," you would no doubt expect me to arrive in a reasonable length of time. You would not expect me to come two thousand years later (but arrive with rapidity once I get there!). This makes absolutely no sense! Jesus, to make His point clear, uses the same imminent time references both *at the beginning and at the end* of Revelation:

> **Rev. 3:11** *Behold,* **I come quickly***: hold that fast which thou hast, that no man take thy crown.* (Emphasis added)

> **Rev. 22:6-7** *And he said unto me, These sayings are faithful and true: and the Lord God of the holy prophets sent his angel to shew unto his servants the things which must* **shortly** *be done.* [7]***Behold, I come quickly****: blessed is he that keepeth the say-*

---

[2] Jack Van Impe, *Jack Van Impe Prophecy Bible*, (Jack Van Impe Ministries International, Troy, MI,)Revelation Revealed, p.3

ings of the prophecy of this book. (Emphasis added)

Rev. 22:10-12 *And he saith unto me,* **Seal not the sayings of the prophecy of this book: for the time is at hand.** [11]*He that is unjust, let him be unjust still: and he which is filthy, let him be filthy still: and he that is righteous, let him be righteous still: and he that is holy, let him be holy still.* [12]*And, behold,* **I come quickly**; *and my reward is with me, to give every man according as his work shall be.* (Emphasis added)

Rev. 22:20 *He which testifieth these things saith,* **Surely I come quickly.** *Amen. Even so, come, Lord Jesus.* (Emphasis added)

To Seal Or Not To Seal?

Another example of this careless misuse of time references is shown in the inconsistent interpretation of the time landmarks used in Daniel and Revelation. Both books give clear evidence regarding the time of their expected fulfillment.

Remember Daniel said, *"Seventy weeks are determined upon thy people and upon thy holy city, to finish the transgression, and to make an end of sins, and to make reconciliation for iniquity, and to bring in everlasting righteousness, and to seal up the vision and prophecy, and to anoint the most Holy."* (Dan 9:24) Daniel's prophecy concerned a 490 year period that would conclude God's dealing with the Jews and Jerusalem (*"upon thy people and upon thy holy city"*). It happened just as predicted with the Jerusalem and the Temple destroyed and the Jews scattered among the nations in 70 A.D. It began and ended in *one generation*, just as Jesus said it would.

Daniel was given instruction concerning the timing and relevance of his prophecy. *"In the third year of Cyrus king of Persia* **a thing was revealed** *unto Daniel, whose name was called Belteshazzar; and the thing was true, but* **the time appointed was long***: and he understood the thing, and had understanding of the vision."* (Dan 10:1)

Later, Daniel was told because of the *"long"* time span that the book was to be sealed until its fulfillment. *"But thou, O Daniel,* **shut up the words, and seal the book, even to the time of the end...***"* (Dan 12:4) For a book to be *"sealed"* meant that *it was not to be understood* by the readers of that day because the fulfillment was a long time away. It was then repeated that the long time span would end with the destruction of the whole Jewish system: *"...when he shall have accomplished to scatter the power of the holy people, all these things shall be finished."* (Dan 12:7) followed by another command to seal the book until the end (the end of the time of God's dealing with the Jew): *"And he said, Go thy way, Daniel: for* **the words are closed up and sealed till the time of the end.***"* (Dan 12:9)

Now compare that with the use of time and seals in Revelation:

> *And he said unto me, These sayings are faithful and true: and the Lord God of the holy prophets sent his angel to show unto his servants the* **things which must shortly be done***. Behold,* **I come quickly***: blessed is he that keepeth the sayings of the prophecy of this book. And I John saw these*

things, and heard them. And when I had heard and seen, I fell down to worship before the feet of the angel which showed me these things. Then saith he unto me, See thou do it not: for I am thy fellow servant, and of thy brethren the prophets, and of them which keep the sayings of this book: worship God. And he saith unto me, **SEAL NOT THE SAYINGS OF THE PROPHECY OF THIS BOOK: FOR THE TIME IS AT HAND.** *He that is unjust, let him be unjust still: and he which is filthy, let him be filthy still: and he that is righteous, let him be righteous still: and he that is holy, let him be holy still. And,* **behold, I come quickly**; *and my reward is with me, to give every man according as his work shall be.* (Rev 22:6-12) (Emphasis added)

Now consider the use of the time references in these two books. Daniel's prophecy was written between 700 and 630 B.C., with its fulfillment taking place in 70 A.D., a length of 700 to 770 years. For the sake of argument let's just call it about 700 years. The scripture says this length of time (700 years) is *"long"* and for that reason the book is to be *"sealed."*

The Book of Revelation was written between 64-68 A.D. Jesus said repeatedly not to seal the book because *"the time is at hand."* Other terms, such as *"soon,"* and *"quickly"* and *"shortly"* are used in the same context. For a book *not* to be *"sealed"* meant that it was *meant to be understood in the time that it was written.* The letters to the seven churches in Revelation were written to churches that physically existed in that day, who surely would understand what Christ was saying to them.

Now unless I'm missing something in my understanding of time relationships, **shortly is shorter than long**! Yet the dispensationalist insists that the events in Revelation are yet future (at this point, we are almost two thousand years future from the time of its writing). If there is any consistency in the time references of the Bible (and there is) this cannot be possible. *Short is not longer than long!*

On the other hand, these time references are consistent with, and pose no problem to, the postmillennialist. They understand the Millennium began with Christ's Ascension in the 1st century and that the judgment of the Jews and Jerusalem foretold in the Revelation actually *did take place "shortly"* just as Jesus said it would. They also understand Daniel's prophecy of the *"time determined"* for the Jewish people, their system of worship, and Jerusalem and the Temple *did already actually take place in the same generation that Jesus was crucified.* Again, this took place in exactly the way and in the time frame predicted by both Daniel and Jesus. It is a seamless eschatology with no great leaps of logic required!

What About the "Last Days?"

As long as we are discussing time and time references there is another important point that must be considered, the meaning of *"the last days"* or *"last times"* mentioned in scripture. Dispensationalists constantly refer to it as an accomplished fact that *"We are living in the last days."* We will again prove conclusively, from the scriptures, that this is not true. **The fact is the *"last days"* ended with the destruction of Jerusalem in 70 A.D.; we are now living in the *"latter days."***

This idea of imminent judgment on the Jews and Jerusalem was an ever present expectation of the New Testament writers and saints. They fully believed Jesus' prophecy of imminent judgment on the apostate Jews, and expected a judgment upon them that was unprecedented in history. They did not expect Jesus to return physically in their lifetime, but they did expect to see him return *"coming on clouds of judgment."*[3] Jesus told them to expect it in their lifetime. *"When you are persecuted in one place, flee to another. I tell you the truth,* **you will not finish going through the cities of Israel before the Son of Man comes.***"* (Mat 10:23 NIV) (Emphasis added)

These were the *"last days,"* the *last generation* (30-70 A.D.) of the Jewish people's position of divine favor, with Jerusalem and the Temple physically existing. They were not the *last days of man's existence before the physical coming of the Lord.*

Scripturally speaking we are living in the *"latter days,"* the time predicted as the time of the *exclusion of Israel from God's plan* while the gospel expands into the whole earth during the *"time of the Gentiles"* (Luke 21:24). *"And it shall come to pass* **in the latter days***, that the mountain of the Lord's house shall be established in the top of the mountains, and shall be exalted above the hills; and all nations shall flow unto it."* (Isa 2:2 NKJV) Consider these scriptures referring to the time *after* the "last days:"

> *For I know that after my death ye will utterly corrupt yourselves, and turn aside from the way which I have commanded you; and* **evil will befall**

---

[3] The meaning of this will be discussed in detail in the next chapter, *A Relevant Revelation.*

*you in the **LATTER DAYS**; because ye will do evil in the sight of the* LORD, *to provoke him to anger through the work of your hands.* (Deut. 31:29) (Emphasis added)

*For I know that my redeemer liveth, and that **he shall stand at the LATTER DAY upon the earth**:* (Job 19:25)

The anger of the LORD *shall not return, until he have executed, and till he have performed the thoughts of his heart: **in the LATTER DAYS ye shall consider it perfectly**.* ²¹*I have not sent these prophets, yet they ran: I have not spoken to them, yet they prophesied.* ²²*But if they had stood in my counsel, and had caused my people to hear my words, then they should have turned them from their evil way, and from the evil of their doings.* (Jer. 23:20-22)

***Afterward** shall the children of Israel return, and seek the LORD their God, and David their king; **and shall fear the* LORD *and his goodness in the LATTER DAYS**.* (Hosea 3:5)

*Now the Spirit speaketh expressly, that **in the LATTER TIMES** some shall depart from the faith, giving heed to seducing spirits, and doctrines of devils;* (1 Tim 4:1)

Most importantly, the New Testament writers were expecting it to take place in a reasonably short period of time, the *"...upon this generation..."* that Jesus had told His disciples they would see. In Matthew 24 He gave them specific things to look for that would precede this judgment and allow them to escape. This sense of imminent judgment and the beginning of something new permeates the whole New Testament:

The night is far spent, ***the day is at hand****: let us therefore cast off the works of darkness, and let us put on the armor of light.* (Rom 13:12)

God, who at sundry times and in divers manners spake in time past unto the fathers by the prophets, Hath ***in these last days*** *spoken unto us by his Son, whom he hath appointed heir of all things, by whom also he made the worlds;* (Heb 1:1-2)

Not forsaking the assembling of ourselves together, as the manner of some is; but exhorting one another: and so much the more, as ***ye see the day approaching****.* (Heb 10:25)

Be patient therefore, brethren *(*living at that time*),* ***unto the coming of the Lord****. Behold, the husbandman waiteth for the precious fruit of the earth, and hath long patience for it, until he receive the early and latter rain.* (James 5:7)

Be ye also patient; stablish your hearts: for ***the coming of the Lord draweth nigh****.* (James 5:8)

But ***the end of all things is at hand****: be ye there-

fore sober, and watch unto prayer. (1 Pet 4:7)

*Little children, **it is the last time**: and as ye have heard that Antichrist shall come, even now are there many antichrists; whereby we know that **it is the last time**.* (1 John 2:18)

*Blessed is he that readeth, and they that hear the words of this prophecy, and keep those things which are written therein: **for the time is at hand.*** (Rev 1:3)

I am sure you get the point. The writers knew they were living in an incredibly important generation, one that would see a *sea change* in God's dealing with humanity. They would see Israel and the Jews phased out and the world and the Gentiles phased in. And they knew that *it all would happen in one generation!*

CHAPTER 7

A Relevant Revelation

Rev. 1:1, 3 (NLT)

> *This is a revelation from Jesus Christ, which God gave him concerning the **events that will happen soon**. An angel was sent to God's servant John so that John could share the revelation with God's other servants...God blesses the one who reads this prophecy to the church, and he blesses all who listen to it and obey what it says. **For the time is near when these things will happen.*** (Emphasis added)

This chapter will consider the dispensationalist's use of Revelation as a guide to the future, rather than its intended application to the saints in the 1st century, who were living *in the Tribulation during the reign of the*

Antichrist.

Considering the scripture quoted above and many other witnesses, there can be no question that Jesus expected an imminent fulfillment of the prophecies of Revelation. In fact, it was given to the Church in the 1st century to give them hope and to serve as a guide to survive the Tribulation which they were *already personally experiencing.* David Chilton, one of the foremost experts on Revelation writes,

> *...the Book of Revelation is primarily a prophecy of the destruction of Jerusalem by the Romans.*[1]

The classic perspective of Christianity is that Revelation is largely historic and mostly depicts the destruction of Jerusalem in a symbolic way. Among those who hold this view are Adam Clarke, John A. T. Robinson, Jay E. Adams, Alfred Edersheim, Joseph Lightfoot, Sir Issac Newton and Robert Young, as well as Holman's Bible Dictionary and many other authoritative sources.

In This Generation

This view accords perfectly with Jesus' clear teaching to His disciples that His return in clouds of judgment[2] would

---

[1] David Chilton, *The Days of Vengeance, An Exposition of the Book of Revelation,* (Dominion Press, Ft. Worth, TX, 1987), p.4 I encourage the reader to examine this book, which, in the author's opinion, is probably the clearest verse by verse exposition of Revelation ever written.

[2] The last indicator of judgment would be *"...the Son of Man coming on the clouds of heaven with power and great glory..."* (Matt. 24:30) The use of the term *"in the clouds"* was typical biblical language for God's judgment from heaven, which men could recognize by its devastating effect on earth. (cp. Exod. 19:7-20, Psa. 18:4-19, 97:1-6, Isa. 19:1, Matt. 26:59-65, Rev. 14:14-20). Lam. 2:1-17 graphically pictures this judgment, which was visited on Jerusalem in 70 A.D.

be during the same generation in which He walked on earth. These words were fulfilled in the destruction of Jerusalem in 70 A.D.

Matthew 23:36, 24:33-34 (NLT)

> *I assure you, all the **accumulated judgment of the centuries** will break upon the heads of **this very generation**.* (Emphasis added)

> *Just so, **when you see** the events I've described beginning to happen, you can know **his return is very near, right at the door**. I assure you, **this generation will not pass from the scene** before all these things take place.* (Emphasis added)

What they would see would be the terrible penalty for their rejection of the Messiah take place in every horrible detail. They had violated their covenant with God, and now were to have the curse for violating the covenant come upon them. The "blessings and curses" of the covenant were detailed in Deuteronomy 28 and 29.

Deut. 29:21-22, 25, 27-28

> *The Lord will separate them from all the tribes of Israel, to pour out on them all the **covenant curses** recorded in this Book of the Law. Then the generations to come, both your own descendants and the foreigners who come from distant lands, **will see the devastation of the land** and the diseases the Lord will send against it.*

*And they will be told, 'This happened because the people of the land **broke the covenant** they made with the Lord, the God of their ancestors, when he brought them out of the land of Egypt.*

*That is why the Lord's anger burned against this land, **bringing down on it all the curses recorded in this book**. ²⁸In great anger and fury the Lord uprooted his people from their land and exiled them to another land, where they still live today!'* (Emphasis added)

The final and most terrible curse was spelled out in Deut. 28:49-57. It would come upon them exactly as predicted:

*The Lord will bring a **distant nation**³ against you, swooping down upon you **like an eagle**;⁴ a nation whose language you don't understand— a nation of fierce and angry men who will have no mercy upon young or old. They will eat you out of house and home until your cattle and crops are gone. Your grain, new wine, olive oil, calves, and lambs will all disappear. That nation will lay siege to your cities and knock down your highest walls— the walls you will trust to protect you. **You will even eat the flesh of your own sons and daugh-***

---

³ Rome. The detail of this prophecy and its exact fulfillment in 70 A.D. is amazing.

⁴ The eagle was the symbol of Rome. An eagle was actually on the ensign or banner of the Roman troops. It represented Rome and it's Caesars as being divine. The eagle ensign was planted in the Holy Place as Jerusalem was taken. This utter desecration of the Temple was called *"the abomination of desolation."* (Dan. 12:11)

> *ters in the terrible days of siege that lie ahead.* The most tenderhearted man among you will be utterly callous toward his own brother and his beloved wife and his children who are still alive. **He will refuse to give them a share of the flesh he is devouring—the flesh of his own children—** because he is starving in the midst of the siege of your cities. The most tender and delicate woman among you—the one who would not so much as touch her feet to the ground—will refuse to share with her beloved husband, son, and daughter. **She will hide from them the afterbirth and the new baby she has borne, so that she herself can eat them:** so terrible will be the hunger during the siege and the awful distress caused by your enemies at your gates. (Deut. 28:49-57 TLB) (Emphasis added)

Jesus indicated that people who had seen Him minister (those living in the generation from 30-70 A.D. would be alive and physically present to see Him return in clouds of judgment pronounced from heaven:

> ...Then the high priest asked him, "Are you the Messiah, the Son of the blessed God?" ^{62}*Jesus* said, "I am, and **you will see me**, the Son of Man, sitting at God's right hand in the place of power and **coming back on the clouds of heaven.**" Mark 14:61-62 (NLT) (Emphasis added)

Included in that group who would see his judgment in 70 A.D.:

> *Behold, he cometh with clouds; and every eye shall see him, and **they also which pierced him:**...* Rev. 1:7 (Emphasis added)

Even as Christ was on His way to be crucified, He reminded the daughters of Jerusalem what would befall them *in their lifetime:*

> *And there followed him a great company of people, and of women, which also bewailed and lamented him. But Jesus turning unto them said, Daughters of Jerusalem, weep not for me, but **weep for yourselves, and for your children**. For, behold, the days are coming, in the which they shall say, Blessed are the barren, and the wombs that never bare, and the paps which never gave suck. Then shall they begin to say to the mountains, Fall on us; and to the hills, Cover us. For if they do these things in a green tree, what shall be done in the dry?* (Luke 23:27-31) (Emphasis added)

Dispensationalists are also very aware of the damage the *"this generation"* statements of Jesus do to their system. In response, they say that the Greek word used for *generation* is *"genea"* which means *"a period of time,"* but could also refer to a *"nation or race."* The only problem with the argument is the word is used 16 times in the New Testament and

---

[5] Finis Jennings Dake, who *is* a dispensationalist, writes in his *Annotated Reference Bible*, *"Occurs 16 times and always of a particular span of life and not of a race of people."* (Dake Bible Sales, Inc., P.O. Box 625, Lawrenceville, GA, 1963), New Testament, p.11, note i, clarifying the use of *"generation"* in Matt. 11:16

[6] Ibid. New Testament, p.26, note c

always refers to a particular span of life and not of a race of people. [5]

It Is Finished

When Jesus' uttered His last cry, *"It is finished..."* in John 19:30, He used a Greek word signifying what a general would say looking over a field where a battle had just been won. In effect it meant, *"The battle is won, all that remains is mopping up!"* In this case it referred to the end (or mopping up) of the whole Jewish system. Dake writes about the desolation Jesus spoke of in Matt:23:

> *Referring to the nation as well as the temple... (There are) Three reasons why the temple was destroyed: 1) Because of their sins. 2) To take away all possibility of continuing Judaism. 3) To prove conclusively that the law was abolished, the old Jewish economy was brought to an end, and the Christian dispensation was introduced.*[6]

The whole scenario, from beginning to "mopping up" was foretold clearly by Daniel in his landmark prophecy:

> *Seventy weeks are determined upon thy people and upon thy holy city,* **to finish** *the transgression, and to* **make an end of sins,**[7] *and to* **make recon-**

---

[7] *"To reserve sins for punishment."* See Matt. 23:29-39 This was the seventh and final stage of judgment contained in the "curse of the law" (Deut. 28:47-67). It was consummated in 70 A.D. for the Jews continual violation of the law. I recommend actual reading of this text to see the actual horrors that took place in Jerusalem in 70 A.D.

ciliation for iniquity,[8] *and to* **bring in everlasting righteousness,**[9] *and to* **seal up the vision and prophecy,**[10] *and to* **anoint the most Holy.**[11] (Dan 9:24) (Emphasis added)

Revelation was a highly symbolic picture of what would take place in Jerusalem in the last of the last days. It was written in symbolic language so it would not be understood by either the Jews or the Roman government, who were both about to be dealt with by God. It was actually written during the Tribulation, a time of intense persecution for the Church, to encourage them that the worst was almost over, and that deserved judgment on their wicked oppressors was going to be withheld no longer. *"And they cried with a loud voice, saying,* **How long***, O Lord, holy and true, dost thou not judge and avenge our blood on them that dwell on the earth? And white robes were given unto every one of them; and it was said unto them, that* **they should rest yet for a lit-**

---

[8] *"For if, when we were enemies, we were reconciled to God by the death of his Son, much more, being reconciled, we shall be saved by his life. And not only so, but we also joy in God through our Lord Jesus Christ, by whom we have now received the atonement."* (Rom. 5:10-11) Also 2 Cor. 5:18-19

[9] Charles Spurgeon, the "Prince of Preachers," commented on this verse, *"One of the main designs of Christ's coming to earth was to bring in everlasting righteousness."*

[10] By the time that this prophecy was fulfilled, with the desolation of Jerusalem, so too, the entire canon of scripture (vision and prophecy) was completed (sealed) with the writing of Revelation.

[11] *"That word, I say, ye know, which was published throughout all Judaea, and began from Galilee, after the baptism which John preached; How God anointed Jesus of Nazareth with the Holy Ghost and with power: who went about doing good, and healing all that were oppressed of the devil; for God was with him."* (Acts 10:37-38) Cp. Matt. 3:13-17, Luke 3:21-24

tle season, until their fellow servants also and their brethren, that should be killed as they were, should be fulfilled." (Rev 6:10-11) (Emphasis added)

In The Tribulation

In the last chapter we looked at several scriptures in Revelation which talked about its soon fulfillment. Jesus used the words *soon, near and at hand*. Other internal references in Revelation also indicate that the book was written specifically to the generation that was then alive. For example, John himself recognized he was *in the Tribulation:*

> *I, John, both your brother, and* **companion in the tribulation,** *and kingdom and patience of Jesus Christ, was in the island that is called Patmos, for the word of God, and for the testimony of Jesus Christ.*[12] (Rev 1:9 NKJV) (Emphasis added)

The reference to *"tribulation"* was also repeated in the letters to the churches at Smyrna and Thyatira (Rev. 2:9-10, 22) which were physically existent in that day. Thyatira was told, *"But that which ye have already hold fast till I come."* (Rev 2:25) (Emphasis added) He could not have meant, speaking to physically present people, that they would *"hold fast till He came"* if His coming was going to be at least *two thousand years in the future*. It makes perfect sense if He was coming in clouds of judgment in just a few years!

Other internal evidence indicates the exact time that Revelation was written. Consider this very revealing pas-

---

[12] Some translations omit the *"the,"* but an examination of the Greek original texts indicate the article is present in the text, and should be so translated, as it is in the New King James Version.

sage: *"And here is the mind which hath wisdom. The **seven heads are seven mountains**, on which the woman sitteth. And **there are seven kings: five are fallen, and one is, and the other is not yet come; and when he cometh, he must continue a short space.**"* (Rev 17:9-10) (Emphasis added) Concerning the *"seven mountains"* Gentry writes:

> *Perhaps no point is more obvious in Revelation than this one: Rome is symbolized here by the seven mountains. Rome is the one city in history that has been distinguished for and universally recognizable by its seven hills. The famous seven hills are the Palatine, Aventine, Caelian, Esquiline, Viminal, Quirinal, and Capitoline hills.*[13]

Even more interesting is the identity of the *"seven kings."* The context makes it clear that they are kings of Rome, or the Roman empire. Her kings were called *Caesars*. Historically, we know without a doubt who they were *and can name them*. Consider Chilton's commentary on Rev. 17:9-10:

> *The angel turns to speak of the Dragon's incarnation in the Beast from the Sea.* **Here is the mind which has wisdom. The seven heads are seven mountains on which the woman sits.** *The seven mountains again identify the Beast as Rome, famous seven mountains for its "seven hills"; but these also correspond to the line of the Caesars,* **for they are seven kings; five have fallen:** *The first five Caesars were Julius, Augustus, Tiberius,*

---

[13] Kenneth L. Gentry, *Before Jerusalem Fell, Dating the Book of Revelation* (Institute for Christian Economics, Tyler, TX, 1989), p.149

Caligula, and Claudius. **One is:** *Nero, the sixth Caesar, was on the throne as St. John was writing the Revelation.* **The other has not yet come; and when he comes, he must remain a little while:** *Galba, the seventh Caesar, reigned for less than seven months.*[14] (Emphasis added)

Again we have a perfect fit with scripture, both its historical and geographical accuracy, and fulfillment. We don't have to speculate about the meaning of a symbolic text two thousand years after the events indicated have taken place. The reader's of John's day understood the symbolism, and that the predicted events would take place shortly, just as Jesus said they would: *"If you read this prophecy aloud to the church, you will receive a special blessing from the Lord. Those who* **listen to it** *being read and* **do what it says** *will also be blessed.* **For the time is near when these things will all come true.***"* (Rev 1:3 TLB) (Emphasis added)

The Antichrist

Speaking of speculation, probably nothing in the word of God has gendered more wild speculation than the identity of the Antichrist. Stalin, Hitler, Mussolini, Henry Kissinger and others have been considered candidates for this nefarious title. Almost all dispensational writers think he is alive today, only waiting to be revealed after the Rapture. But again they have been confused by the "gap" that doesn't exist. The early church knew who the Antichrist was *because they read the book of Revelation where his identity was revealed!*

---

[14] David Chilton, *The Days of Vengeance, An Exposition of the Book of Revelation,* (Dominion Press, Ft. Worth, TX, 1987), p.435-436

Remember, Revelation, according to Jesus' own words, was written to a living generation that would see it literally come to pass before their eyes. This point cannot be emphasized too strongly. This also means that the "common man" would also have the knowledge to understand the metaphors and symbolism in their day.

For example, we in the 21st century understand the meaning of *"PC's"* (personal computers) They are common to our age and understanding. Yet if you were to go back in time to only 1975, and started talking about *"PC's"* no one would have a clue about what you were talking about because they weren't invented yet. But what if you were to go two thousand years into the future? Would anyone then (unless they were a history buff) have any idea what a *"PC"* was? Probably not! Why? Because technology will have advanced far beyond personal computers by that time.

The 1st century Christian had understanding that we do not have. And it was to this group of people, *and their understanding*, that Revelation was written. And it is for this reason that we, two thousand years later, have such a difficult time understanding the almost completely symbolic book of Revelation. It was not meant for us to understand in the same way that they did. We can learn spiritual lessons about God and His attitude toward sin and the devil from Revelation, but for them it was a matter of encouragement and literal, physical, survival in a very dangerous time.

With that understanding in mind let's consider the Antichrist. In our day almost everyone, saint and sinner alike, has heard he can be identified by a number, 666. We struggle to figure out what that means. Some have said it relates to computer codes. Others have said it has to do with the number of letters in a person's name. Some pointed to

President Reagan, since his name, Ronald Wilson Reagan, was three names of six letters or "666." That numeric identifier is taken from the book of Revelation: *"Here is wisdom. Let him that hath understanding count the number of the beast: for it is the number of a man; and his number is Six hundred threescore and six."* (Rev 13:18)

Again, Revelation was written for the people who were alive at the time of its writing. They *thought in terms of letters and numbers*, so identifying a person with a number was a natural thing for them to do;

> **In Hebrew (as in most ancient languages), the alphabet served double duty: each letter was also a numeral. Thus any given word or group of words had a numerical value, which could be computed simply by adding up the numerals.** *The language-system of the West avoids this by using the Roman alphabet for its letters and the Arabic alphabet for its numerals. It is thus difficult and artificial for us to imagine going back and forth between the letter-use and numeral-use of the characters in our language, but for the ancients it was quite natural. In all probability, they did not need to engage in any great mental shifts back and forth, but simply saw and comprehended both aspects at once.*[15] (Emphasis added)
>
> *As we have already noted, the ancient languages used each letter of the alphabet as a numeral as*

---

[15] David Chilton, *The Days of Vengeance, An Exposition of the Book of Revelation,* (Dominion Press, Ft. Worth, TX, 1987), p.346

well; thus, the number of anyone's name could be computed by simply adding up the numerical value of its letters. **Clearly, St. John expected that his contemporary readers were capable of using this method to discover the Beast's name — thus indicating, again, the contemporary message of Revelation; he did not expect them to figure out the name of some 20th-century official in a foreign government.** At the same time, however, he tells them that it will not be as easy as they might think: it will require someone "who has understanding." For St. John did not give a number that could be worked out in Greek, which is what a Roman official scanning Revelation for subversive content would expect. The unexpected element in the computation was that it had to be worked out in Hebrew, a language that at least some members of the churches would know. His readers would have guessed by now that he was speaking of Nero, and those who understood Hebrew probably grasped it instantly. The numerical values of the Hebrew letters in Neron Kesar (Nero Caesar) are 666.

As I mentioned earlier, the point is not that Nero's name is the primary identification of 666. The point is, instead, what the number meant to the churches. St. John's Biblically informed readers will have already recognized many clear indications of the Beast's identity as Rome (indeed, they already knew this from reading the Book of Daniel). Now Nero has arrived on the scene as the

> *first great persecutor of the Church, the embodiment of the "666-ness" of the Empire, and - Lo and behold!—his very name spells out 666.* It is significant that "all the earliest Christian writers on the Apocalypse, from Irenaeus down to Victorinus of Pettau and Commodian in the fourth, and Andreas in the fifth, and St. Beatus in the eighth century, connect Nero, or some Roman emperor, with the Apocalyptic Beast. **There should be no reasonable doubt about this identification. St. John was writing to first-century Christians, warning them of things that were "shortly" to take place.**[16] (Emphasis added)

Notice how perfectly the symbolism fit the understanding of the 1st century Christian. To him it made perfect sense, whereas to us (as so many have proved) it is a complete mystery. It is just as Jesus said, *"And he saith unto me, Seal not the sayings of the prophecy of this book: for the time is at hand."* (Rev 22:10) **It was not sealed *from them* because it was written *to them* and the understanding they had.** Chilton is not the only one who holds this view:

> *In Revelation 13, the "first beast" must be considered both generically and specifically. This is not unusual in Scripture: Christ's body is generic (the Church) and specific (Jesus); Adam is generic (man) and specific (Adam). Generically the "Beast" is Rome; specifically it is Nero Caesar, the head of the Roman Empire of the day.*

---

[16] Ibid. p.350-351

The rationale for the generic identity is as follows. The time frame of the book is supportive of the identification (see earlier argumentation). The Beast rises from the sea, which suggests the Italian peninsula where Rome is located, when considered from the vantage of either Patmos or Israel (across the Mediterranean Sea). It has "seven heads" (Rev. 13: 1; 17:3) that are "seven mountains" (Rev. 17:8,9); Rome is famous for its "Seven Hills." Specifically, Beast = Nero. **The Beast's number is an exercise in Hebrew gematria: converting letters into numbers. An ancient Hebrew spelling of Nero Caesar perfectly fits the value: "Nrwn Qsr" (Rev. 13:18): n [50] r [200] w [6] n [50] q [100] s [60] r [200].** *Its evil and blasphemous character suggests Nero specifically, and the emperors generically: Since Julius Caesar, the emperors were often considered divine. Roman historian Dio Cassius records of Nero's return to Rome from Greece: "The people cried out: 'Thou august, august! To Nero, the Hercules! To Nero, the Apollo! The Eternal One! Thou august! Sacred voice! Happy those who hear thee!'" In addition, Nero was the first emperor to persecute Christianity (13:7), and he did so for a period of forty-two months (Nov.* A.D. *64 to June* A.D. *68, Rev. 13:5).*[17] (Emphasis added)

It is not the intent of this book to do a comprehensive exposition of Revelation. Chilton has already done an excel-

---

[17] Kenneth L. Gentry, *He Shall Have Dominion* (Institute for Christian Economics, Tyler, TX, 1992), p.409

lent job. Suffice it to say that *the rest of Revelation can also be explained in the light of historic events that took place in the 1st century*, just as we have done with the Tribulation and the Antichrist. The point I'm trying to make is that Revelation was relevant to contemporary 1st century Christians. To shift its fulfillment two thousand years or more into the future, as the dispensationalists do, certainly cannot be justified by the clear language of the text itself or any other portion of scripture. *The events foretold in Revelation were relevant to the 1st century, not the 21st century!*

CHAPTER 8

When Will These Things Be?

Matthew 24:3 (NLT)

> Later, Jesus sat on the slopes of the Mount of Olives. His disciples came to him privately and asked, **When** will all this take place? And **will there be any sign** ahead of time to signal **your return** and **the end of the world?** (Emphasis added)

The hallmark of the dispensationalist is his use of today's headlines as "proof" of fulfillment of biblical prophecy. Some calamitous event takes place in the world (or especially Israel) and he cries, *"See, the Lord's return is near, just as He said it would be!"* And usually his frame of reference is what Jesus said to His disciples in Matthew 24.[1] Unfortunately, this is a complete violation of the text and what Jesus was saying to His disciples. And again, as we have seen repeatedly, it utterly disregards the plain "time stamp" Jesus put on His prophetic declaration.

The Setting For Jesus' Prophecy

The reason for Jesus' explanation to His disciples in Matthew 24 actually begins with Jesus denunciation of Jerusalem and the Jewish scribes and Pharisees that began in Matthew 23 and concluded with these words of *imminent impending judgment* upon them, Jerusalem, and the Temple:

> ***Woe unto you, scribes and Pharisees, hypocrites!*** *because ye build the tombs of the prophets, and garnish the sepulchers of the righteous, And say, If we had been in the days of our fathers, we would not have been partakers with them in the blood of the prophets. Wherefore ye be witnesses unto yourselves, that ye are the children of them which killed the prophets. Fill ye up then the measure of your fathers.*
>
> *Ye serpents,* ***ye generation of vipers****, how can ye escape the damnation of hell? Wherefore, behold,* ***I send unto you*** *prophets, and wise men, and scribes: and* ***some of them ye shall kill*** *and crucify; and* ***some of them shall ye scourge in your synagogues****, and* ***persecute them*** *from city to city:*

---

[1] Parallel passages of the Olivet Discourse are found in Mark 13 and Luke 21.

THAT UPON YOU *may come all the righteous blood shed upon the earth, from the blood of righteous Abel unto the blood of Zacharias son of Barachias, whom ye slew between the temple and the altar.* ***VERILY I SAY UNTO YOU, ALL THESE THINGS SHALL COME UPON THIS GENERATION.***

*O **Jerusalem, Jerusalem**, thou that killest the prophets, and stonest them which are sent unto thee, how often would I have gathered thy children together, even as a hen gathereth her chickens under her wings, and ye would not! Behold, your house is left unto you **desolate**. For I say unto you, Ye shall not see me henceforth, till ye shall say, Blessed is he that cometh in the name of the Lord.* (Matt. 23:29-39) (Emphasis added)

Jesus was simply restating the magnitude of the judgment that would be seen when He came *"...in clouds of judgment..."* in order to usher in the Kingdom of God. He had spoken of this time before, but not with such clarity and detail. And, as we have said repeatedly, He spoke of this as **something that would happen to the generation of people to whom He spoke.** Here are two examples of Jesus instructing His disciples *about what they would face before He returned to judge their persecutors:*

*Behold, **I send you** forth as sheep in the midst of wolves: be ye therefore wise as serpents, and harmless as doves. But beware of men: for they will deliver you up to the councils, and they will* *scourge you in their synagogues;* ***And ye*** *shall be brought before governors and kings for my sake, for a testimony against them and the Gentiles. But when* ***they deliver you up****, take no thought how or what ye shall speak: for* ***it shall be given you*** *in that same hour what ye shall speak. For it is not ye that speak, but the Spirit of your Father which speaketh in you. And the brother shall deliver up the brother to death, and the father the child: and the children shall rise up against their parents, and cause them to be put to death.* ***And ye*** *shall be hated of all men for my name's sake: but he that endureth to the end shall be saved. But when they persecute you in this city, flee ye into another: for verily I say unto you,* **<u>YE SHALL NOT HAVE GONE OVER THE CITIES OF ISRAEL, TILL THE SON OF MAN BE COME.</u>** (Matt. 10:16-23) (Emphasis added)

And also:

For the Son of man shall come in the glory of his Father with his angels; and then he shall reward every man according to his works. Verily I say unto you, **<u>THERE BE SOME STANDING HERE, WHICH SHALL NOT TASTE OF DEATH, TILL THEY SEE THE SON OF MAN COMING IN HIS KINGDOM.</u>** (Matt. 16:27-28) (Emphasis added)

After Jesus' severe statements of woe to the scribes and Pharisees, Jesus and His disciples left the Temple. His disciples, awed with the magnificence of the Temple, offered to give Jesus a guided tour. Jesus' response to them again reinforced the immanence and severity of the judgment that would come *in their lifetime:*

> *And Jesus went out, and departed from the temple: and his disciples came to him for to show him the buildings of the temple. And Jesus said unto them,* **See ye not all these things?** *verily I say unto you,* **THERE SHALL NOT BE LEFT HERE ONE STONE UPON ANOTHER, that shall not be thrown down.** (Matt. 23:29-24:2) (Emphasis added)

The Three Questions

No doubt His disciples were too shocked to respond to this statement, and His earlier statement in the Temple. At first they tried to figure it out, but later an opportunity came to ask Jesus privately what He meant. They asked Him *three questions about what He had said:*

> *And as he sat upon the mount of Olives, the disciples came unto him privately, saying, Tell us,* **when shall these things be?** *and* **what shall be the sign of thy coming, and of the end of the world?** (Matt. 24:3) (Emphasis added)

The first two questions related specifically to the disciples and what they would *personally* observe. The first, *"When will these things be?,"* referred especially to *when* the *"not one stone will be left upon another,"* comment would come to pass. The second question, *"What will be the sign of thy coming?,"* was a request for information about signs *they personally would see* immediately before Jesus came in clouds of judgment to bring utter desolation to the Jews, Judaism, Jerusalem and the Temple.

The third question, *"What will be the sign of the end of the world?,"* was a request for information about any signs or events by which the Jesus disciples (or anyone else) could know that the end of the world or the end of time was approaching. The very fact that they asked the questions separately is a clear indication that Jesus disciples knew there would be *a significant time span* between Jesus' *coming in clouds of judgment in their generation*, and ***a later physical coming AT THE END OF TIME.***

The Time Stamp

Of primary importance in the study of the Jesus' prophetic remarks in Matthew 24 is the "time stamp" that Jesus placed on their fulfillment. Just as Jesus "time stamped" the Revelation with His *"at hand," "quickly," "soon,"* and *"shortly"* statements at **both the beginning and end of Revelation** so there would be no mistake as to when it would happen, so too, *He "time stamped" both the beginning and end of the events that those listening to Him would see in their lifetime.*

The beginning *"in this generation"* statement is made in Matt. 23:36: *"Verily I say unto you, All these things shall come upon this generation."* The closing "time stamp" for the answers to the first two questions is found in Matt. 24:34: *"Verily I say unto you, **This generation shall not pass**, till all these things be fulfilled."* **Therefore, *everything Jesus spoke about between Matthew 23:36 and Matthew 24:34, had to be things that the disciples would personally***

witness. They have *absolutely no relevance* to today's events happening two thousand years later! It also might be added that the Temple that was to be so completely destroyed *was the Temple they had just visited, not some future Temple. And it was completely destroyed in 70* A.D.*!*

What Would They See?

> *And Jesus answered and said unto them, Take heed that no man deceive you. For many shall come in my name, saying, I am Christ; and shall deceive many.* (Matt. 24:4-5)

The dispensationalist attempts to apply this scripture to today's headlines as "signs of the imminent rapture." Cult leaders like Sun Myung Moon and David Koresh are mentioned as false Christs, and hence, signs of the coming end. In truth, these false Messiahs did manifest in the times of the disciples and therefore warranted Jesus' word of caution.

Notice Jesus warning *"...that no man deceive you..."* followed by the comment that *"many"* would be deceived. The deception of these false Messiahs was a danger to His disciples, that *they* might be deceived. He also said there would be *"many"* of these deceivers. While we may have to contend with Rev. Moon and other cult leaders, we could hardly say there are many of them. Neither do they pose much of a threat of deception to genuine believers due to their bizarre doctrines. But according to Jesus' own statement these impostors would be *many and dangerous.*

This word *was relevant to His disciples.* Remember, in Jesus' day, because of Daniel's prophecy dating the time of Messiah's physical incarnation, people were looking for the

Messiah. They knew the time that Daniel had predicted was very near. As I mentioned in Chapter 3, Anna, Simeon, and many others were *"looking for the redemption of Israel."* This expectation, in effect, opened the door for false Messiahs to proclaim their identity. And because people were expecting Messiah in that day, it served to disarm them of some of the "buyer's resistance" which would normally have lead them to disregard these claims as fanatical.

History bears out the claim that this is exactly what occurred in the period between 30 and 70 A.D.:

> *History records but few of the names of those who claimed to be the Messiah in the period from the ascension of Jesus Christ to the destruction of Jerusalem. Undoubtedly many were too insignificant to be recorded by historians. But we do have allusions to those who tried to deceive the people by their claims. For instance, as early as in Acts 8:9-10 we read concerning a Simon Magus: "But there was a certain man, called Simon, which before time in the same city used sorcery, and bewitched the people of Samaria, giving out that himself was some great one: to whom they all gave heed, from the least to the greatest, saying, This man is the great power of God." Several of the early Christian writers refer to Simon Magus. Justin relates that, in the time of Claudius Caesar, Simon was worshiped as a god at Rome on account of his magical powers. Jerome quotes Simon Magus as saying, "I am the Word of God, I am the Comforter, I am Almighty, I am all there is of God" (Mansel, The Gnostic Heresies, p. 82).*

> *And Irenaeus tells us how Simon claimed to be the Son of God and the creator of angels.*
>
> *Origen informs us of a Dositheus who claimed that he was the Christ foretold by Moses. The historian Josephus describes the time of Felix as mentioned in Acts: "**Now as for the affairs of the Jews, they grew worse and worse continually, for the country was again filled with robbers and impostors, who deluded the multitude.** Yet did Felix catch and put to death many of those impostors **every day**, together with the robbers." **This gives some idea of the number of persons who sought to deceive the multitudes with their false claims.** To protect his followers from such impostors, Jesus foretold them and warned against being deceived by their claims.*[2]

Signs of the Times

Again it is clear that Jesus' remarks had current application to the disciples who personally heard His words. The same is true of the next statement of times and signs that were to precede the Desolation.

> *And ye shall hear of wars and rumors of wars: see that ye be not troubled: for all these things must come to pass, but the end is not yet. For nation shall rise against nation, and kingdom against kingdom: and there shall be famines, and pestilences, and earthquakes, in divers places. All*

---

[2] J. Marcellus Kik, *An Eschatology of Victory*, (Presbyterian & Reformed Publishing, Phillipsburg, NJ), p.91-92

these are the beginning of sorrows. (Matt. 24:6-8)

This passage of scripture must be interpreted in the context of the "time stamp" Jesus placed on it, the *"this generation"* to whom he was speaking. It could not possibly refer to future generations, including ours, since *"wars and rumors of wars"* have occurred frequently and almost continually since Jesus' statement declaring them to be *"the beginning of sorrows."* This fact would have rendered His words almost without meaning. But the fact is, the statement did have meaning to His disciples, since *they were living in a period of extended peace*, the Pax Romana, which extended for over sixty years from the time of Jesus' birth.

> *We read in the next verses of "wars and rumors of wars" (Matt. 24:6-7a). These serve as signs of the end of the Temple because of the dramatically successful Pax Romana.* **Origen** (A.D. **185-254) speaks of the "abundance of peace that began at the birth of Christ"** *(Origen, Romans 1:3). Historians observe that "in the Roman Empire proper,* **this period of peace remained comparatively undisturbed until the time of Nero.** *It was ruptured with the outbreak of the Jewish War and the Roman Civil Wars in the violent Year of Four Emperors* (A.D. *68-69), which for Rome "was almost the end. (Tacitus, Histories 1:11).*
>
> **In Matthew 24:7-11, many woes are prophesied. All of these woes are abundantly accounted for in the events of the era leading up to the crisis of** A.D. **70: *famines, pestilences, earthquakes, perse-***

*cution, apostasy, and false prophets.*³

Kik gives more evidence concerning the accuracy of Jesus' prophecy:

> *The beginning of sorrows for the Jewish nation would consist of wars, famines, pestilences, and earthquakes. All these things would occur sometime previous to the destruction of Jerusalem.* **At the time Jesus revealed this state of affairs, the Roman Empire was experiencing peace within its borders.** *However, it was not long after the Olivet Discourse that strife, insurrections, and wars were filling both Palestine and other parts of the Roman Empire. In Rome itself, four emperors came to a violent death in the short space of eighteen months. Were one to give account of all the disturbances that actually occurred within the Empire after Jesus' death, he would be constrained to write a separate book.*
>
> *To the Jews it was a highly turbulent time. There was an uprising against them in Alexandria. In Seleucia 50,000 were slain. In Caesaria a battle between Syrians and Jews brought death to about 20,000 Jews. The fight between Syrians and Jews divided many villages and towns into armed camps.* **Constant rumors of wars kept the Jewish people in an unsettled state.** *Josephus mentions how Caligula, the Roman Emperor, made orders*

---

³ Kenneth L. Gentry, *He Shall Have Dominion* (Institute for Christian Economics, Tyler, TX, 1992), p.344

that his statue be placed in the Temple of Jerusalem. Because the Jews refused to allow this, they lived in constant fear that the Emperor might send an army into Palestine. **Some Jews lived in such fear that they dared not even plow and seed the ground.**

*Acts 11:28 makes mention of a **famine** which occurred in the day of Claudius Caesar.* **It was a famine that spread not only in Judea but other parts of the world, and like all famines, it was followed by pestilences that caused the death of thousands.** *And as to **earthquakes**, many are mentioned by writers during a period just previous to 70* A.D. *There were earthquakes in Crete, Smyrna, Miletus, Chios, Samos, Laodicea, Hierapolis, Colosse, Campania, Rome, and Judea. It is interesting to note that the city of Pompeii was much damaged by an earthquake occurring on February 5, 63,* A.D.

From the above evidence one may conclude that the prophecy of Jesus was literally fulfilled as to wars, famines, pestilences, and earthquakes. Christ told his disciples that they were not to be troubled by these things because these calamities did not indicate the end. Throughout history there have been those who have taken these signs as indicating the approaching end of the world. Even today, national and international calamities are said to be decisive proofs that the world is coming to its end. The Lord, however, teaches that these signs did not even mean the end of Jerusalem. He says, "But the end is not yet." Hence the disciples were not to be troubled when they beheld these events.[4]

Again, Jesus' words prove to be accurate and relevant to the people He told would see all of these signs in their generation.

Then shall they deliver you up to be afflicted, and shall kill you: and ye shall be hated of all nations for my name's sake. (Matt. 24:9)

Now the focus of Christ's comments turn to what the Church would experience prior to the coming judgment on Jerusalem and the Jews. The "all nations," of course refer to the nations of the Roman Empire. A quick look at the book of Acts confirms the accuracy of the prophecy. The Apostles were beaten and imprisoned, Stephen was stoned, James was put to death by Herod, and there was great persecution against the Church in Jerusalem. (Acts 8:1)

And then shall many be offended, and shall betray one another, and shall hate one another. (Mat 24:10)

The scriptures also give ample evidence to the truth of this word of warning: *"This thou knowest, that all they which are in Asia be turned away from me; of whom are Phygellus and Hermogenes."* (2 Tim 1:15) *"For Demas hath forsaken me,*

---

[4] J. Marcellus Kik, *An Eschatology of Victory*, (Presbyterian & Reformed Publishing, Phillipsburg, NJ), p.92-93

having loved this present world, and is departed unto Thessalonica; Crescens to Galatia, Titus unto Dalmatia. At my first answer no man stood with me, but all men forsook me: I pray God that it may not be laid to their charge." (2 Tim 4:10, 16)

During the persecution begun by Nero it became common for Christians to betray one another. Tacitus, the Roman historian, records, *"that several Christians at first were apprehended, and then, by their discovery, a multitude of others were convicted, and cruelly put to death, with derision and insult."* [5]

> *And many false prophets shall rise, and shall deceive many.* (Matt. 24:11)

Again, the scriptures well document the war against false prophets that took place in the book of Acts. Their errant doctrines were refuted in the epistles.

> *For I know this, that after my departing shall grievous wolves enter in among you, not sparing the flock.* (Acts 20:29)

> *Now I beseech you, brethren, mark them which cause divisions and offences contrary to the doctrine which ye have learned; and avoid them. For they that are such serve not our Lord Jesus Christ, but their own belly; and by good words and fair speeches deceive the hearts of the simple.* (Rom 16:17-18)

---

[5] Ibid. p.95

> *Beloved, believe not every spirit, but try the spirits whether they are of God: because many false prophets are gone out into the world.* (1 John 4:1)

What is amazing is not that all of these events occurred, but that they occurred in a specific generation, the one that Jesus was addressing in His Olivet Discourse. That is why *it should be obvious to all* that this section of scripture was *addressed to the generation who heard it spoken*, not to one thousands of years into the future.

> *And because iniquity shall abound, the love of many shall wax cold.* (Mat 24:12)

We often think of the 1st century Church as being "perfect," but that was far from the fact. They too, had to be exhorted to live out the faith they professed. The church at Ephesus, existent in the 1st century, was warned to return to its first love: *"Yet I hold this against you: You have forsaken your first love. Remember the height from which you have fallen! Repent and do the things you did at first. If you do not repent, I will come to you and remove your lampstand from its place."* (Rev 2:4-5 NIV) This was symptomatic of the age:

> *During this period there would not only be danger from false prophets, but the influence of prevalent wickedness dampening Christian zeal and love. Christ had indicated that the love of many would wax cold because of the prevalence of iniquity. This does not speak of apostasy but rather of spiritual deterioration.* **The Epistles give abundant evidence of the decrease of spirituality on the**

part of the churches. This was the burden of many Epistles. *Again and again Paul had to admonish the Christians for their lack of zeal and love and for their lack of discernment. Hebrews 10:25 indicates that many forsook the assembling of themselves together for public worship. In Galatians 3:1-4 Paul complains that the foolish Galatians were soon bewitched by false prophets. To Timothy Paul revealed how the love of the world had caused Demas to leave him.*[6]

But he that shall endure unto the end, the same shall be saved. (Matt. 24:13)

One of the most remarkable facts concerns the escape of Christians from Jerusalem prior to its destruction. It is estimated that over one million people died in the siege and overthrow of the city, *but not one Christian died.* The reason for this remarkable fact is that the Christians heeded the warnings of scripture in Matthew, Mark, Luke and Revelation and escaped the unbelievable carnage. The historical record of what happened in Jerusalem in the Great Tribulation is horrible. Here is but one example of what happened while Jerusalem was under siege:

Josephus recounts a story about a wealthy and cultured woman that will illustrate the truth that Christ's description of the terrible tribulation was not extravagant. *This woman had stored up a great deal of food. But during the siege, she was*

---

[6] Ibid. p.96

robbed of all that she had. Cursing the villains in her despair, "she then attempted a most unnatural thing: and snatching up her son, who was a child sucking at her breast, she said, 'O thou miserable infant: for whom shall I preserve thee in this war, this famine, and this sedition? As to the war with the Romans, if they preserve our lives, we must be slaves. This famine also will destroy us, even before than slavery comes upon us. Yet are these seditious rogues more terrible than both the other. Come on; be thou my food, and be thou a fury to these seditious varlets and a by-word to the world, which is all that is now wanting to complete the calamities of us Jews.' As soon as she had said this, she slew her son, and then roasted him, and ate the one-half of him, and kept the other half by her concealed. Upon this the seditious came in presently, and smelling the horrid scent of this food, they threatened her that they would cut her throat immediately if she did not show them what food she had gotten ready. She replied that she had saved a very fine portion of it for them, and withal uncovered what was left of her son. Hereupon they were seized with a horror and amazement of mind, and stood astonished at the sight, when she said to them, 'This is mine own son, and what hath been done was mine own doing! Come, eat of this food; for I have eaten of it myself. Do you not pretend to be either more tender than a woman, or more compassionate than a mother; but if you be so scrupulous, and do abominate this my sacrifice, as I have eaten the onehalf, let the rest be reserved for me also.' After which those men went out trembling, being never so much affrighted at anything as they were at this, and with some difficulty they left the rest of that meat to the mother.

In the light of this and other things too horrifying to mention it is no wonder that Christ wept as he thought of this tragedy, and cried out to the wailing women of Jerusalem, *"Daughters of Jerusalem, weep not for me, but weep for yourselves, and for your children. For, behold, the days are coming, in the which they shall say, Blessed are the barren, and the wombs that never bare, and the paps which never gave suck."*[7] He *was not* speaking to people two thousand or more years into the future, but rather to the people who were physically under the sound of His words.

All of the events mentioned in Matt. 24:3-14 were to occur before the coming of the Lord (not physically, but in "clouds of judgment) to end the age of the Jew and Israel. The last of these "signs of the times" would be the delivery of the gospel message to the known "world," all the nations that were submitted to the Roman empire. *"And this gospel of the kingdom shall be preached in all the world for a witness unto all nations; and then shall the end come."* (Matt. 24:14) Scripture and history again record the fact that this actually occurred before 70 A.D., and before the end of the writing of the New Testament.

The word "world" (oikumene) often stands for the Roman Empire (Luke 2:1; Acts 11:28; 24:15). The

---

[7] Ibid. p.113-115

> phrase "all the nations," is epexegetical, referring to those nations that were subsumed under the imperial authority of Rome. The world to which the "gospel of the kingdom was preached" was provided a witness: "the gospel which has come to you, as it has also **in all the world**.... The gospel which you heard, which was preached to **every creature under heaven**" (Col 1:6, 23; cf Acts 2:5; Rom. 1:8; 10:18).[8]

Specific Warnings and Instructions

Following the instruction concerning general things that would be observable by the disciples begins a section that describes in clear detail what they would see just prior to the time when *"not one stone would be left upon another."*

> *When ye therefore shall see the abomination of desolation, spoken of by Daniel the prophet, stand in the holy place, (whoso readeth, let him understand:) Then let them which be in Judaea flee into the mountains: Let him which is on the housetop not come down to take any thing out of his house: Neither let him which is in the field return back to take his clothes. And woe unto them that are with child, and to them that give suck in those days! But pray ye that your flight be not in the winter, neither on the sabbath day: For then shall be great tribulation, such as was not since the beginning of the world to this time, no, nor ever shall be. And except those days should be shortened, there*

---

[8] Kenneth L. Gentry, *He Shall Have Dominion* (Institute for Christian Economics, Tyler, TX, 1992), p.344

should no flesh be saved: but for the elect's sake those days shall be shortened. (Matt. 24:14-22)

Even the admonition *"whoso readeth, let him understand"* speaks to the fact that Jesus intended His remark to be understood by a living generation. The key event that they were to look for was *"the abomination of desolation, spoken of by Daniel the prophet, stand in the holy place..."* Again, this was an event *they would see.* And again, the event actually took place in September of 70 A.D.

Dispensationalists believe this event to be the Antichrist himself entering the Temple, but in fact this is not what is predicted. Notice the language of the text. *"When ye therefore shall see the **abomination of desolation**, spoken of by Daniel the prophet, **stand** in the holy place..."* The "abomination of desolation" was not a person, but a thing and an event. It was the placing and worship of the Roman *eagle ensign* (which represented the Roman Caesar as god) in the Temple and *offering worship to him.*

> *During the days leading up to Jerusalem's final destruction, revolution was stirred within the city which resulted in "the outer Temple [being] all of it overflowed with blood" (Wars 4:5:1; cf. 5:1:1-3; 5:13:6).*
>
> *Ultimately, of course, Titus' victory is completed. Upon that victory the Romans burned "the holy house itself, and all the buildings lying round about it, brought their ensigns to the Temple, and set them over against its eastern gate; and there did they offer sacrifices to them" (Wars 6:6:1). It*

was particularly distressing to the Jew that the abominable Gentile (Acts 10:28; 11:2-3; cf Eph. 2:14) would ultimately enter into the Temple of God. The "abomination of desolation" involves the destruction of Jerusalem (beginning with its encircling) and culminates in this final abominable act.

The eagles and lightning. This very conclusion seems to be in Christ's mind, when Christ states: "For wherever the carcass is, there the eagles [*aetos*] will be gathered together" (Matt. 24:28 NKJV). The Roman ensigns set up by Titus in the holy of holies in the Temple were eagles (*Wars* 3:6:2). According to verse 27, the coming of the Roman armies under the direction of Christ (Matt. 22:7) is a death-dealing, destructive judgment coming on Israel "like lightning."

Time To Escape!

During this time immediately preceding the fall of Jerusalem there would be many impostors. *They were expecting a physical coming of the Messiah to rescue them from this terrible calamity. But Christ was clear that He was not coming physically, nor was He going to deliver them, but rather was going to send the Roman army to inflict judgment on them.* So He instructs His disciples not to be taken in by these false prophets and impostor Messiahs. The key event, which would come like a lightning bolt, will be the "abomination of desolation." When *they see it*, it will signal imminent and almost immediate destruction and death. At that point they must take flight and escape. Even the reference to the rooftops was meaningful to the disciples. The houses were built with flat roofs and in close proximity to each other. Therefore it was possible for them to flee Jerusalem without leaving the rooftops, which would be their avenue of escape. Historically that is what actually occurred, and, as a result, not a single Christian died in the fall of Jerusalem!

> *Then if any man shall say unto you, Lo, here is Christ, or there; believe it not. For there shall arise false Christs, and false prophets, and shall show great signs and wonders; insomuch that, if it were possible, they shall deceive the very elect. Behold, I have told you before. Wherefore if they shall say unto you, Behold, he is in the desert; go not forth: behold, he is in the secret chambers; believe it not. For as the lightning cometh out of the east, and shineth even unto the west; so shall also the coming of the Son of man be. For wheresoever the carcase is, there will the eagles be gathered together.* (Matt. 24:23-28)

The comments about "the desert" and "secret chambers" again reinforce the local and immediate nature of Jesus' remarks. Finally, Jesus speaks to the incredible spiritual and symbolic significance of the events that would take place in 70 A.D.

> *Immediately after the tribulation of those days shall the sun be darkened, and the moon shall not give her light, and the stars shall fall from heaven, and the powers of the heavens shall be shaken: And then shall appear the sign of the Son of man*

in heaven: and then shall all the tribes of the earth mourn, and they shall see the Son of man coming in the clouds of heaven with power and great glory. And he shall send his angels with a great sound of a trumpet, and they shall gather together his elect from the four winds, from one end of heaven to the other. (Matt. 24:29-31)

A Darkened Sun?

It should be obvious His comments are allegorical rather than literal. For example, if the sun were to go dark for any length of time earth would turn to ice and all life would die. Or if a star (the sun is a star) were to fall to earth, earth would be incinerated. What is being referred to is a calamitous event among the nations. Israel was to fall from its position as "God's favorite" and be treated worse than the Gentiles, who were now to be favored. This type of language is used elsewhere in scripture to describe the fall of mighty nations. Consider the fall of Egypt predicted by Ezekiel:

Ezekiel 32:2, 7-8

Son of man, take up a lamentation for Pharaoh king of Egypt, and say unto him, Thou art like a young lion of the nations, and thou art as a whale in the seas: and thou camest forth with thy rivers, and troubledst the waters with thy feet, and fouledst their rivers...[7] And when I shall put thee out, I will cover the heaven, and make the stars thereof dark; I will cover the sun with a cloud, and the moon shall not give her light. [8] All the bright lights of heaven will I make dark over thee, and set darkness upon thy land, saith the Lord God.

Gentry also comments on this use of terminology:

The darkening of the sun and moon is common apocalyptic language for the collapse of nations, *such as in Old Testament judgments on Babylon (Isa. 13:1, 10, 19), Idumea (Isa. 34:3-5), Israel Jer. 4:14, 16, 23ff, Joel 2: 10-11), and Egypt (Ezek. 32:2, 7-8, 11-12). This interpretation of the apocalyptic language of these passages is not exceptional. Even allegedly literalistic dispensationalists can write of Isaiah 13:10: "The statements in 13:10 about the heavenly bodies ... no longer function may figuratively describe the total turnaround of the political structure of the Near East. The same would be true of the heavens trembling and the earth shaking (v. 13), figures of speech suggesting all-encompassing destruction." He (John A. Martin) figured it out.*

The final collapse of Jerusalem and the Temple will be the sign that the Son of Man, whom the Jews rejected and crucified, is in heaven (Matt. 24:30). The fulfillment of His judgment word demonstrates His heavenly position and power. This causes the Jewish tribes of the Land (ge) to mourn (kopto, cf. Luke 23:27-28). Through these events the Jews were to "see" the Son of Man in His judgment—coming in terrifying cloud-glory: clouds are symbols of divine majesty often entail-

ing stormy destruction (Isa. 19:1; cf. Psa. 18:10-14; Lam. 2:1; Ezek. 30:3-5). The members of the Sanhedrin and others would experience such in their life times (Matt. 26:64; Mark 9:1; cf. Rev. 1:7 with Rev. 1:1, 3).[9]

A Final Time Stamp

Now learn a parable of the fig tree; When his branch is yet tender, and putteth forth leaves, ye know that summer is nigh: So likewise ye, when ye shall see all these things, know that it is near, even at the doors. Verily I say unto you, **This generation shall not pass, till all these things be fulfilled.** *Heaven and earth shall pass away, but my words shall not pass away.* (Matt. 24:32-35)

Jesus, in concluding His final answer to their first two questions (*"****When*** *will all this take place? And* ***will there be any sign*** *ahead of time to* ***signal your return***...") uses a natural illustration to give them a time frame. In this part of the country (Wisconsin) we know it is a sure sign of spring when we see the robins appear. He told them, in the same way, that they know that when the fig tree puts forth leaves, summer is imminent. He then gave them two unmistakable clues. When they saw the detailed signs He had just described (especially the "abomination of desolation"), they would know that Christ's return in judgment was very near, and so should take appropriate action. He also *specifically limited the length of time until it would occur*—**this gener-**

---

[9] Ibid, p.348

ation! *The ones who were hearing Him speak* would see everything He predicted come to pass. ***History verifies the fact that all the things He spoke did occur just as He said they would.***

An Incredible Parallel

We have previously documented the relevancy of the book of Revelation to the 1st century Christian. It, along with the Olivet Discourse, was a survival guide to the Tribulation. What is incredible (although it could be expected) is the parallel between the warnings of Matthew and Revelation. The seven seals of Revelation chapter six exactly match the warnings of Jesus in Matthew.

Matthew 24 plainly forms a perfect parallelism to the six seals, not only of its *events*, but also in *the order of their occurrence*: 24:3, the first seal, the white horse bringing the conquering Roman army; 24:6, the second seal, the red horse taking away peace ; 24:7, the third seal, the black horse bringing famine; 24:7, the fourth seal, the pale horse of death; 24:9, the fifth seal, including evil persecutions, judgments, and gospel preaching to all nations (24:9-28); 24:29, the sixth seal, phenomena in the heavens signifying the end of Israel's prominence among the nations.

Was this an accident? I think not! *What Christ described literally in Matthew, He described symbolically in Revelation!* Both were clear warnings, instructions, and encouragement for the saints, that the end of the evil system that persecuted them was near. Again, the scriptures and their historical fulfillment concur exactly, to the smallest detail!

The Last Question

> *...**will there be any sign** ahead of time to signal...**the end of the world**?* (Matt. 24:3b NLT)

There is a stark contrast between the *specific details* given in Matt. 24:3-35, and the *lack of detail* given in Matt. 24:36-44. The first section describes in increasing detail when they will see the destruction of Jerusalem, including a key event to look for, the abomination of desolation. The later section gives no detail, and specifically says there will be *no sign* of its impending occurrence. The reason should be obvious. *The answer is different because the question is different!* Jesus now begins to answer *the third question* posed to Him in Matt. 24:3b, *"...**will there be any sign** ahead of time to signal...**the end of the world**?"*

> *But **of that day and hour knoweth no man**, no, not the angels of heaven, but my Father only. But as the days of Noe were, so shall also the coming of the Son of man be. For as in the days that were before the flood they were eating and drinking, marrying and giving in marriage, until the day that Noe entered into the ark, And **knew not** until the flood came, and **took them all away**; so shall also the coming of the Son of man be. Then shall two be in the field; the one shall be taken, and the other left. Two women shall be grinding at the mill; the **one shall be taken, and the other left**. Watch therefore: for **ye know not** what hour your Lord doth come. But know this, that if the goodman of the house had known in what watch the*

*thief would come, he would have watched, and would not have suffered his house to be broken up. Therefore be ye also ready: **for in such an hour as ye think not the Son of man cometh.*** (Matt 24:36-44)

Notice the dramatic change! From giving them signs that all of them could see, and so, *would know what was about to occur,* now He tells them that *no one would know when this event would occur.* He changed His answer because He is now answering a different question! The first two questions were about *the age they were living in*, the last question was about *the end of the age to come*. The end of that age would be *the end of time*, when Christ would return *physically* to complete the Redemption of the saints and to judge the wicked.

Who Is Left Behind?

An interesting fact about this passage is the *"...one shall be taken, and the other left..."* language. While some may claim this refers to the "rapture," consistent dispensationalists realize this (according to their own system) is not possible because of their "gap" or "mystery" doctrine. They teach that none of the prophets "saw" the Church Age (of which the "rapture" is the last event) including Jesus, who was in effect an Old Testament dispensation prophet. The "rapture" could only be revealed in the Church Age (the Epistles). According to dispensationalists, Christ could not here be referring to the "rapture" because *even He did not know about it.*

Then what is He referring to? Think about it. In the days of Noah, who was taken and who was left? The sinners were taken by death, Noah and his family were the ones who were "left behind" (sounds like a good title for a *fiction* book!) *to inhabit and repopulate the earth!* This is consistent with other biblical statements. Take for example Jesus interpretation of the parable of the wheat and tares:

> *Then Jesus sent the multitude away, and went into the house: and his disciples came unto him, saying, Declare unto us the parable of the tares of the field. He answered and said unto them, He that soweth the good seed is the Son of man; The field is the world; the good seed are the children of the kingdom; but the tares are the children of the wicked one; The enemy that sowed them is the devil;* **the harvest is the end of the world; and the reapers are the angels.** *As therefore the tares are gathered and burned in the fire;* **so shall it be in the end of this world.** *The Son of man shall send forth his angels, and* **they shall gather out of his kingdom all things that offend, and them which do iniquity;** *And shall cast them into a furnace of fire: there shall be wailing and gnashing of teeth. Then shall the righteous shine forth as the sun in the kingdom of their Father. Who hath ears to hear, let him hear.* (Matt. 13:36-43)

It is amazing! The dispensationalist is always trying to get the saints out, the Lord is always *keeping the saints in* and *removing the wicked by death!* Consider this: *"The righteous shall never be removed: but the wicked shall not inhabit the earth."* (Prov 10:30) Or better yet Jesus' own words: *"****I pray not*** *that thou shouldest take them out of the* *world, but that thou shouldest keep them from the evil."* (John 17:15) How do you think the Kingdom of God will prosper and be the major influence in the whole earth, with the saints in or out? The answer should be obvious!

His Final Answer

It is so plain, therefore it is hard to understand how this passage has been so badly misinterpreted. The disciples last question, *"...will there be any sign ahead of time to signal...the end of the world?"* Jesus' final answer was an emphatic *"No!"* There will be *no signs.* There will be *no warnings. No one, including the angels, will know the day or hour.* It will come as a complete and total surprise to everyone on the face of the earth!

Think about it. Of all the "prophecy experts," beginning with William Miller who predicted the Lord's return in 1844, Darby, (*"The Lord will unquestionably return in 1867."*), Billy Graham, 1952, Hal Lindsay, 1981, Edgar Whisenant, 1988, (who, when it didn't happen, *"recalculated"* the return in 1989), and many since, *not one of them has been right!* And none will ever be right because the Lord Himself said, *"But of that day and hour knoweth no man, no, not the angels of heaven, but my Father only."* If that was the Lord's *"final answer"* it should be ours too!

CHAPTER 9

The Prophets Have Spoken

> *Now change your mind and attitude to God and turn to him so he can cleanse away your sins and send you wonderful times of refreshment from the presence of the Lord and **send Jesus** your Messiah back to you again. For **HE <u>MUST REMAIN</u> IN HEAVEN** until the final recovery of all things from sin, as prophesied from ancient times.* Acts 3:19-21 (TLB)

The New Testament Church had a clear understanding of eschatology from its earliest days. Here, in the second recorded sermon, Peter declared *the Lord **must remain in heaven** until the final recovery of all things from sin*. He also declared that the extent of that recovery had been the subject of things the prophets had spoken from ancient times. If that be the case, then we can look to what the prophets have spoken to give us a clear understanding of *what must occur before Jesus can leave heaven and return to earth.*

We know from the scriptures that the last event in *"the final recovery of all things from sin"* is the elimination of death. *"Then the end will come, when he hands over the kingdom to God the Father after he has destroyed all dominion, authority and power. For he must reign until he has put all his enemies under his feet. The* **last enemy** *to be destroyed is* **death.**" (1 Cor. 15:24-26 NIV).

Death is the enemy that was invited into the earth by the sin of Adam. It is the wages of sin. It will be in the earth as long as man is on the earth. Only when Christ returns will it be eliminated. But *until* Christ returns to eliminate death He will *reign from heaven* until His other enemies are dealt with by the Church empowered by the Holy Spirit.

What Does The Millennium Look Like?

What would happen in the earth during the Millennium (the time of Christ's reign) was the subject of many prophetic utterances. The prophets, by the Spirit of God, looked into the future to see what Christ's reign would produce in the earth. And they described certain events, often in metaphoric terms, that would characterize what the earth would look like as Christ's reign from heaven came to full fruition on the earth. And remember, *until these events came to pass on earth,* **Christ must remain in heaven.**

Isaiah 2:1-4

> *The word that Isaiah the son of Amoz saw concerning Judah and Jerusalem.* ²*And it shall come to pass in the latter days, that the mountain of the*

LORD'S house shall be established on the top of the mountains, and shall be exalted above the hills; and all nations shall flow unto it. ³And many people shall go and say, Come ye, and let us go up to the mountain of the LORD, to the house of the God of Jacob; and he will teach us of his ways, and we will walk in his paths: for out of Zion shall go forth the law, and the word of the LORD from Jerusalem. ⁴And he shall judge among the nations, and shall rebuke many people: and they shall beat their swords into plowshares, and their spears into pruninghooks: nation shall not lift up sword against nation, neither shall they learn war any more.

Isaiah 9:6-7

For unto us a child is born, unto us a son is given: and the government shall be upon his shoulder: and his name shall be called Wonderful, Counsellor, The mighty God, The everlasting Father, The Prince of Peace. **⁷*Of the increase of his government and peace there shall be no end*,** *upon the throne of David, and upon his kingdom, to order it, and to establish it with judgment and with justice from henceforth even for ever.* **The zeal of the LORD of hosts will perform this.**

Isaiah 11:1-10

And there shall come forth a rod out of the stem of Jesse, and a Branch shall grow out of his roots:

²And the spirit of the LORD shall rest upon him, the spirit of wisdom and understanding, the spirit of counsel and might, the spirit of knowledge and of the fear of the LORD; ³And shall make him of quick understanding in the fear of the LORD: and he shall not judge after the sight of his eyes, neither reprove after the hearing of his ears: ⁴But with righteousness shall he judge the poor, and reprove with equity for the meek of the earth: and he shall smite the earth with the rod of his mouth, and with the breath of his lips shall he slay the wicked. ⁵And righteousness shall be the girdle of his loins, and faithfulness the girdle of his reins. ⁶The wolf also shall dwell with the lamb, and the leopard shall lie down with the kid; and the calf and the young lion and the fatling together; and a little child shall lead them. ⁷And the cow and the bear shall feed; their young ones shall lie down together: and the lion shall eat straw like the ox. ⁸And the sucking child shall play on the hole of the asp, and the weaned child shall put his hand on the cockatrice' den. **⁹They shall not hurt nor destroy in all my holy mountain: for the earth shall be full of the knowledge of the LORD, as the waters cover the sea.** *¹⁰And in that day there shall be a root of Jesse, which shall stand for an ensign of the people; to it shall the Gentiles seek: and his rest shall be glorious.*

Isaiah 65:20-25

There shall be no more thence an infant of days,

> *nor an old man that hath not filled his days: for the child shall die an hundred years old; but the sinner being an hundred years old shall be accursed.* ²¹*And they shall build houses, and inhabit them; and they shall plant vineyards, and eat the fruit of them.* ²²*They shall not build, and another inhabit; they shall not plant, and another eat: for as the days of a tree are the days of my people, and mine elect shall long enjoy the work of their hands.* ²³*They shall not labor in vain, nor bring forth for trouble; for they are the seed of the blessed of the LORD, and their offspring with them.* ²⁴*And it shall come to pass, that before they call, I will answer; and while they are yet speaking, I will hear.* ²⁵*The wolf and the lamb shall feed together, and the lion shall eat straw like the bullock: and dust shall be the serpent's meat. They shall not hurt nor destroy in all my holy mountain, saith the LORD.*

All of these verses refer to what the earth will "look like" during the time of the Millennium. The knowledge and fear of the Lord will be so expansive that nations (yes, there will still be nations during this time) and people will be at peace to such an extent that warfare will no longer be learned, and weapons will be turned into tools of production instead instruments of destruction. Natural hostilities between nations and races will be removed as His government *progressively increases and the Kingdom of God expands to fill the whole earth.* As the reign of God increases so will the life span of men, so that one who dies at a hundred years old will be considered as one who died as a child (Isa. 65:20).

How Does The "Garden" Grow?

While this may seem incredible, or even impossible, from our point of view, four things must be considered. First, the testimony of Jesus was that this Kingdom would expand so slowly as to be almost unobservable while it was taking place, like leaven in dough. (Luke 13:20-21) *"And again he said, Whereunto shall I liken the kingdom of God? It is like leaven, which a woman took and hid in three measures of meal, till the whole was leavened."*

Second, He also declared that this Kingdom, unlike other kingdoms, would not come with an observable beginning. (Luke 17:20-21) *"And when he was demanded of the Pharisees, when the kingdom of God should come, he answered them and said,* **The kingdom of God cometh not with observation:** *Neither shall they say, Lo here! or, lo there! for, behold, the kingdom of God is within* (Lit. "Among") *you."* **This is absolute proof that the Millennium *will not begin with the physical return of Christ to the earth!*** If that were the case you could definitely refer to a specific time and place of the origin of the Kingdom of God. Instead, as we have seen, Daniel said the Kingdom would begin during the time of Roman government, not with an observable change of political government, but rather beginning in the hearts of men.

Third, Jesus also said, the Kingdom would gradually expand to cover the whole earth. (Luke 13:18-19) *"Then Jesus asked, "What is the kingdom of God like? What shall I compare it to? It is like a mustard seed, which a man took and planted in his garden. It grew and became a tree, and the birds of the air perched in its branches."* Governments and societies take on the character of the subjects they govern. Eventually the Kingdom in the hearts of men will expand to such an extent that it will effect every culture and government. This is what will bring about the universal peace between people and nations.

Fourth, while it may seem that it is impossible for this to occur while sinful men inhabit the earth, it is clear that the scripture says *it will happen!* The word, speaking of the Millennium, declares, *"...the sinner being an hundred years old shall be accursed."* (Isa. 65:20b) The Millennium will have saints and sinners coexisting, but the saints, not the sinners, will gradually gain pre-eminence. How can this even be possible? Again, all we have to do is look to the scriptures to find the answer: *"The zeal of the Lord of hosts will perform this."* (Isa. 9:7) God has not lost His power.

Where Is Christ?

All of the millennial schemes (except amillennialism) expect a Millennium or "Golden Age." The critical distinction between the schemes is *where is Christ while it occurs?* The premillennialist believes Christ must be *physically present on earth.* We have already proved the scriptures refute this idea. The postmillennialist believes *Christ will reign from heaven during the Millennium.* This is what the scripture teaches. The difficulty we have in accepting this truth does not alter the fact that the Bible says *it will occur!*

If God could, *while reigning from heaven,* overthrow Pharaoh and Egypt, He can do it today! If He could, *while reigning from heaven,* cause Nebuchadnezzar, the ruler of the greatest kingdom ever, to eat grass for seven years and then restore him to his throne, He can do it today. If God says He will, *while reigning from heaven,* make His enemies His footstool through His Spirit-empowered Church, then you can be sure He will! (Psa. 110:1-2) *"The LORD said unto my Lord, Sit thou at my right hand, until I make thine enemies thy footstool. The LORD shall send the rod of thy strength out of Zion* (A SYMBOL of God's dwelling place, or for the people of God, i.e. the people among whom God dwells. This was Israel under the Old Covenant and they TYPIFIED the Church under the New Covenant[1]): *rule thou in the midst of thine enemies."*

This sounds much more victorious than Darby's defeatist scheme: *"...**instead of permitting ourselves to hope for a continued progress of good, we must expect a progress of evil**; and that the hope of the earth being filled with the knowledge of the Lord before the exercise of His judgment and the consummation of this judgment on the earth, is delusive. **We are to expect evil**, until it becomes so flagrant that it will be necessary for the Lord to judge it..."*[2] God's plan is to take the earth, not abandon it to the devil and the Antichrist!

Some Dispensational teachers, contrary to their own teaching, remark that Old Testament scriptures about the "millennium" are quoted in the New Testament applying to the Church Age. Remember, the dispensationalist insists the Old Testament prophets did not "see" the Church Age. Bob Yandian, the dispensationalist from whom I learned much of my eschatology while at Rhema Bible Training Center, writes,

---

[1] W. Stuart Owen, *A Dictionary of Bible Symbols* (London, England: Grace Publications Trust, 1992), 148

[2] J. N. Darby in a lecture delivered in Geneva in 1840 on *Progress of Evil on the Earth*. (The Collected Writings of Y. N. Darby, Prophetic, Vol. 1), 471 and 483

> *I used to wonder why **Peter quoted a millennial passage out of the book of Joel** (Acts 2.16,17) **on the day of Pentecost**. Peter quoted that passage because he knew, "Hey folks, we've entered our millennium" "If you've accepted Jesus as your Savior, your millennium has come. The Holy Spirit brought the kingdom to the earth on the Day of Pentecost and we entered into it."[3]*

I suggest why Peter applied a "millennium" scripture to the Church Age is because they are one and the same. His utterance was inspired by the Holy Ghost and recorded in the canon of scripture. It was not a mistake, it was a revelation of truth. We are now living in the Millennium, the space of time in which the gospel will fill the earth and make Christian the nations!

We, as Christians, both individually and collectively, are to do our part to expand the Kingdom of God on earth. We are to do so with the full assurance that we are doing the will of God, and can expect the wind of heaven to be blowing at our back, not in our face. We are to expect and work toward the earth getting progressively better, rather than throwing in our hands and expecting things to get worse and worse. It was this very philosophy that dominated the thinking of the Founders of our country. We will not do any harm if we emulate their efforts! May God give us the grace to return to the expectation and zeal of our fathers.

---

[3] Bob Yandian, *How to Become Great in the Kingdom of God*, (Dallas, TX: Word of Faith Publishing, 1983) 98,99

CHAPTER 10

A Future, A Hope, An Expected End

The kings of the earth, and all the inhabitants of the world, would not have believed that the adversary and the enemy should have entered into the gates of Jerusalem. (Lam 4:12)

For I know the plans I have for you, declares the LORD, *plans to prosper you and not to harm you, plans to give you hope and a future.* (Jer 29:11 NIV)

We now come to the "bottom line." The reason for the writing of this book. The Church today stands at a pivotal point in its journey with God. Much like Israel, we are standing at the doorway of the promised land of milk and honey. We have heard the report of the "twelve spies." The ten (dispensationalists) have told us *"there are giants in the land and they are growing. There is no way we can take the fortified cities of the humanists. We must wait for the Lord to return and rescue us from our enemies, after all, we the Church are only grasshoppers in our sight and in their sight."*

The minority report, given by the two (postmillennialists), stands in stark contrast to the view of the majority. They insist that *God has promised to be with us in battle.* Even though He won't be physically there, *He will be with us, and will send His Holy Spirit to aid us.* In fact, our Lord was so bold as to say, *"But the fact of the matter is that it is best for you that I go away, for if I don't, the Comforter won't come. If I do, he will—for I will send him to you. And when he has come he will convince the world of its sin, and of the availability of God's goodness, and of deliverance from judgment."* (John 16:7-8 TLB) There is no possibility of failure unless we throw in our hand. The conquest of Christ through His Church is inevitable! The only question is will we take part in it, or leave it to future generations to inherit the blessing of Christ? Let us go up at once and take the promised land! If we will go, God will give us victory. Now, as in the days of Israel, the question is, "Whose report will we (the Church) believe?"

This illustration is not as far-fetched as you might think. The dealings of God with Israel, and later the Church, are parallel. Israel was given a promise and a geographical territory (the Promised Land) to subdue. The Church too was given a promise and a geographical territory (the world) to bring under the dominion of Christ. Both were assured of victory if they would only obey.

Even the Old Testament scriptures referred symbolically to the yet future Church as "Zion." As we have noted before, (Psa 110:1-2) *"The LORD said unto my Lord, Sit thou at my right hand, until I make thine enemies thy footstool. The LORD shall send the rod of thy strength out of* **Zion (A SYMBOL of God's dwelling place, or for the people of God, i.e. the people among whom God dwells. This was Israel under the Old Covenant and they TYPIFIED the Church under the New Covenant**[1]): *rule thou in the midst of thine enemies."*

Possessing the Gate of the Enemy

"The kings of the earth, and all the inhabitants of the world, would not have believed that the adversary and the enemy should have entered into the gates of Jerusalem." In Lam. 4:12, Israel issued this **cry of despair** because God had promised to Abraham that his seed **would possess the gates of his enemies** and that **all nations would be blessed** because **he obeyed his voice.** (Gen. 22:12-18)

"Gates" are a seat of authority, a stronghold. In ancient times all cities were walled, and the one who controlled the gate controlled the city. Gates were meant to keep enemies out and let friends in. The "key to the city" was really *the key to the gate of the city, in other words, access at all times.* The gate of the city was also **the place where the *rulers of the city dwelt.*** *"Her husband is **known in the gates**, when he sitteth among the elders of the land."* (Prov. 31:23) Finally, **"gates" signified cultural, social, and political control**. They could be held by either friends or enemies. *"And they*

---

[1] W. Stuart Owen, *A Dictionary of Bible Symbols* (London, England: Grace Publications Trust, 1992), 148

blessed Rebekah, and said unto her, Thou art our sister, be thou the mother of thousands of millions, and let thy seed possess the gate of those which hate them." (Gen 24:60)

What was true in the natural is true in the spiritual; for every city and nation there are various "gates" (financial, political, spiritual, educational, etc.). He who controls those "gates" controls the city. Needless to say, to control the gates is a blessing. And God has always promised to give the "gates" to His people as long as they obeyed Him.

When Israel obeyed God gave them the "turf" (geographical and political control) of their enemies. The enemies either submitted to their rule and were blessed in the blessing of Israel, or were destroyed.[2] When Israel disobeyed, that generation perished, and the promise was left for the next generation.[3] **All this was carried out with God reigning from Heaven.**

It all happened quite literally. The "Wilderness generation" perished, the "Joshua generation" went in and was given **supernatural assistance in subduing her enemies.**[4] Israel disobeyed the command to *"go into the land and possess it"* because they did not believe the word of God or the *"good report."* They chose rather to believe the *"evil report"* of men who did not believe what God had said. They perished because they didn't believe God would perform what He had promised. That is a historical fact![5]

Right now, whether we like it or not, the devil controls most of the "gates" of the city despite God's promise that *"the gates of Hell"* (Matt. 16:13-19) would not prevail

---

[2] See Deut. 7:1-16
[3] See Deut. 8:20
[4] See Deut. 9:1-3, Josh. 21:43-45
[5] See Num. 13:25-33

against the Church. And in good part, the blame for this can be placed at the doorstep of dispensationalism. The majority of the Spirit-filled churches in America have believed the "evil report" that things will get worse and worse, and as a result we have in effect "packed our bags" for the Rapture ride to heaven. What's the use of polishing the brass on a sinking ship?

Philosophies Do Have Consequences!

The philosophies and arguments we believe become strongholds. The Bible tells us to *"tear down strongholds."* The New English Bible says it this way, *"The weapons we wield are not merely human, but divinely potent to demolish strongholds. We demolish sophistries and all that rears its proud head against the knowledge of God. We compel every human thought to surrender in obedience to Christ."* (2 Cor. 10:4-5) Unfortunately, for most of the church, dispensationalism has become a sophistry which needs to be cast down.

We have clearly demonstrated in this book that dispensationalism has no scriptural or historical basis. It is a fabrication of J. N. Darby that has slowed the momentum of the Millennium. It must, and eventually will, be cast off. The only question is whether we will throw it off, and again, as our forefathers did, begin building the Kingdom, or will we die in the Wilderness of Do-Nothing.

> *And Jesus came and spake unto them, saying, All power is given unto me in heaven and in earth. Go ye therefore, and teach all nations, baptizing them in the name of the Father, and of the Son, and of the Holy Ghost: Teaching them to observe all things whatsoever I have commanded you: and,*

> *lo, I am with you alway, even unto the end of the world. Amen.* (Matt. 28:18-20)

They were to consider the whole world as their "turf." *There is something about taking REAL ESTATE that the enemy violently resists!* Matthew Henry's Commentary says this about this verse: *"The principle intention of this commission is to disciple all nations. Admit their disciples.* **Do your utmost to make the nations Christian nations."** When we talk of a Christian nation, this does not mean that everyone, every individual, will submit to Christ's rule. What it means is that the Christian world view, the Christian presupposition, will be the undergirding and overriding mind set of the nation and culture. Charles Wesley said, *"Individual change brings societal change, but if there is no societal change there's been no individual change."* The Lord said He would be *"with us"* until we complete the task! He did not say that He would have to return to either *"rescue us"* or *"to get the job done right."*

It was through believing a "bad report," one contrary to scripture, that we have allowed many of the "gates of the nation" to be taken. That report, issued by J.N. Darby in 1826 began the demise of American Christianity. *But we are not utterly without hope!*

The "good report" is still available for us to believe and act upon. *"And the seventh angel sounded; and there were great voices in heaven, saying,* **The kingdoms of this world are become the kingdoms of our Lord, and of his Christ; and he shall reign for ever and ever."** (Rev. 11:15) It is through revelation and understanding that we will take the "gates" back! Revelation causes a believer to become aggressive. We are to go to the nation and the world in the sure hope of complete victory in earth, while Jesus continues to reign from Heaven!

Destined To Win!

It is us, not the enemy, who are destined to win in history! But we must discard our defensive mentality if we are to *personally* experience victory. God has given authority to prophesy to the gates and establish justice in them. Just like the "gates of communism" fell in a short time, so will these! We are anointed to "take the gates".

The "heroes of faith" listed in Hebrews 11 "subdued kingdoms," but the scripture tells us they are waiting for us to complete the mission! The Kingdom begins in us *invisibly* when we are born again, but that Kingdom is not to remain invisible in us or around us. We are to "bring the reign of the King" to all around us; marriage, family, church, employer, society, government, science and the arts. We are to exert ourselves to bring the Kingdom of God in manifestation to all who see us.

As the Kingdom advances Satan's works will be progressively eliminated. As it was for Israel, so it will be for the Church. In the war with Satan's Kingdom on all fronts, there are no victories without battles. God pledges victory, but victory requires warfare!

Scottish Exegete John Brown wrote, *"It is in the exercise of this power, thus acquired, that He so regulates the rise and decline and fall of empires and the progress of commerce, and science and art, and, indeed, all events...by which, through the accompanying power of the Spirit, the Prince of this world is ultimately to be expelled from every corner of the world, the whole of which, with scarcely an exception, for so many ages, lain completely under his iron yoke."* This vision was the hope of the Great Commission and God's people throughout the ages, until it was dimmed by dispensationalism.

Great Expectations

> *For I know the plans I have for you, declares the LORD, plans to prosper you and not to harm you, plans to give you hope and a future.* (Jer 29:11 NIV)

For any nation in the world to be transformed, those who would do so must be motivated by hope that their plans are to finally succeed. There is no better basis for hope than the word of God. We have shown that it clearly promises a better world before Christ's return. It speaks powerfully against the pessimism of dispensationalism.

The Founders of this nation labored diligently to make America a "city set on a hill" for all nations to observe and emulate. They were not concerned that it might not come to full fruition during their lifetimes. What they were concerned about was that they would leave something behind that their posterity might build upon, until the dream of a world *filled with the knowledge of the Lord as the waters cover the sea"* would be fully realized.

This powerful, motivating, hope of a world under Christ's dominion, that has been nearly extinguished by dispensationalism and "Rapture Fever," can be kindled again by a return to biblically faithful and historically sound postmillennial eschatology, coupled with the Spirit energized works of the saints. It is my prayer that this book will, by the grace of God, serve at least a small part in bringing that to pass.

Selected Bibliography

Chilton, David. *The Days of Vengeance, An Exposition of the Book of Revelation.* Dominion Press, Ft. Worth, TX, 1987.

Gentry, Kenneth L. *Before Jerusalem Fell, Dating the Book of Revelation.* Institute for Christian Economics, Tyler, TX, 1989.

Gentry, Kenneth L. *He Shall Have Dominion.* Institutes for Christian Economics, Tyler, TX, 1992.

Kik, J. Marcellus. *An Eschatology of Victory.* Presbyterian & Reformed Publishing, Phillipsburg, NJ.

Murray, Iain H. *The Puritan Hope, Revival and the Interpretation of Prophecy.* Banner of Truth Trust, Edinburgh, England, 1971.

Owen, W. Stuart. A *Dictionary of Bible Symbols.* Grace Publications Trust, London, England, 1992.

CPSIA information can be obtained
at www.ICGtesting.com
Printed in the USA
FSHW010136170520
70264FS